THE
BIBLE
THE
BASKETBALL
AND THE
BRIEFCASE

THE
BIBLE
THE
BASKETBALL
AND THE
BRIEFCASE

JAY MARTIN

CREATION
HOUSE

THE BIBLE, THE BASKETBALL, AND THE BRIEFCASE
by Jay Martin
Published by Creation House
A Charisma Media Company
600 Rinehart Road
Lake Mary, Florida 32746
www.charismamedia.com

Unless otherwise noted, all Scripture quotations are from the King James Version of the Bible.

Scripture quotations marked NIV are from the Holy Bible, New International Version of the Bible. Copyright © 1973, 1978, 1984, International Bible Society. Used by permission.

The story of Svea Flood and her daughter, Aggie Byrd, may be found in Jim Cymbala, *Fresh Power* (Grand Rapids, MI: Zondervan, 2003).

Millard Fuller's biography is based on "Millard Fuller: Habitat for Humanity International Founder, *Habitat for Humanity*, accessed May 11, 2016, at http://www.habitat.org/how/millard.aspx.

Design Director: Justin Evans
Cover design by Ken McClure

Visit the author's website: wallacelawfirm.com

Library of Congress Control Number: 2016940941
International Standard Book Number: 978-1-62998-556-5
E-book International Standard Book Number:
978-1-62998-557-2

First edition

16 17 18 19 20 — 987654321
Printed in the United States of America

CONTENTS

FOREWORD

by Rev. Rod Loy

THE STORY OF Scripture is that God works in unique ways. He uses ordinary people to do extraordinary things. The key is willing obedience, even when what God asks doesn't seem to make logical sense.

Over two thousand years after the last book of Scripture was written God's methods haven't changed. He still uses the unlikely to do the impossible in His strength and power.

Over fifteen years ago, God spoke to a preppy, comfortable lawyer, challenging him to get out of his comfort zone and love kids and students who were overlooked, unwanted, and unloved. From an inner-city basketball court to what is today Metro Worship Center, Jay Martin has been obedient.

Jay has accumulated a lot of titles: lawyer, successful politician, community leader, and majority leader of the State House of Representatives of Arkansas. But, none of those titles describe Jay as well as his favorite one: pastor.

Metro Worship Center, ministering to the homeless, the hurting, and at-risk students, is not Pastor Jay's dream. It's God's dream, brought to pass because of Jay's dogged determination and dedication to the task.

Over and over I've watched Pastor Jay walk away from career advancement and money-making opportunities in order to spend time in the worst neighborhoods of our city building God's kingdom instead of his own. Jay and his wife, Dawn, and their three girls have aligned their lives so they can say yes to whatever God asks. The results? Children, students, and adults are becoming lifelong followers of Jesus Christ. The long-term impact of the ministry is a joy to see!

My prayer as you read this book is that you will see how one person determined to make a difference can be used in an incredible way. One person obedient to God and willing to sacrifice can change the world.

My prayer goes beyond you seeing that it *can* happen. I want you to be willing to be the one God uses. Your moment of obedience and your life of sacrifice could set in motion something beyond anything you've ever imagined.

The story of Pastor Jay and Metro is more than a story. It's what God wants to do in communities across the country. There's no doubt it's on God's heart. I pray He places it in your heart!

Do you feel ordinary? Do you wonder how God could ever use you to do something magnificent? Get ready! You are just like Pastor Jay Martin! God's got huge plans for your life. I pray you sign up for the adventure of a lifetime and change the world!

—REV. ROD LOY
SENIOR PASTOR, FIRST ASSEMBLY OF GOD
NORTH LITTLE ROCK, AR

FOREWORD

by Dr. Alton Garrison

I N A SURVEY of church attendees 93 percent said they thought it was the responsibility of every Christian to share the gospel with non-Christians, yet just 17 percent felt totally confident they could share their belief in Christ with someone else effectively. If sharing our faith is so important why do so few of us attempt it? Maybe we are afraid of rejection or we feel untrained and inadequate. Some may even think they must possess the gift of evangelism to be successful. Regardless of the obstacles, evangelism does not feel natural or easy to most people.

But what if you took a different approach?

What if you did not try to preach a sermon or share a memorized, predetermined speech? What if you decided to become a friend in just a normal, relaxed way—someone who would care about another person's needs and build a relationship with them?

Jay Martin was one of the most unlikely people to drive into a needy neighborhood, walk out onto a concrete basketball court, and start playing ball with little African-American kids. The trajectory of his life seemed to be leading him in a much different direction. As you read his story you will realize his future seemed destined for a law career, political involvement, and marriage to a beautiful lady, Dawn, a pediatrician.

Yet the tugging in his heart and his obedience to a relentless prompting led him onto a court that day. As his pastor at the time I remember it well. It did not start with a sermon. There certainly was not a Metro Worship Center on the drawing board. Nonetheless, one step motivated simply by caring about inner-city children who needed love, attention, and spiritual direction has resulted in a dynamic ministry to the hurting and hopeless.

The book you are holding could be a textbook for Relationship Evangelism 101. Jay tells moving stories and shares proven principles that will challenge and motivate all of us to begin conversations and build relationships while believing God for redemptive results.

—DR. ALTON GARRISON
ASSISTANT SUPERINTENDENT,
GENERAL COUNCIL OF THE ASSEMBLIES OF GOD

INTRODUCTION

I LOVE STORIES. I love to learn about journeys of faith that people take. As a Christian having felt called to ministry, stories motivate me to further my ministry journey. As an attorney, stories of people who used their profession to help the less fortunate have encouraged me to serve as an attorney who puts public service first.

The story that motivated me the most in my ministry journey was told by my then-pastor, Dr. Alton Garrison, in the late 1990s during a sermon at First Assembly, North Little Rock.

Pastor Garrison told the story of a missionary couple, David and Svea Flood. They were commissioned by their home church in Stockholm, Sweden, and dispatched to a country in Central Africa. The couple left with the hope of establishing churches and communities of faith all over central Africa.

However, the witch doctors in the village in which they were ministering were very powerful. After a year of ministry, loving people in the community and sharing their faith, the Floods still had not established one church or even had one convert to the Christian faith. Yet, they continued loving and serving the families in the village.

One point of hope occurred often when Ms. Flood welcomed a young boy into her home. The boy came by to sell eggs to Ms. Flood. When he came to her home Ms. Flood would place the boy on her lap, hold him, and tell him Bible stories. She looked forward to his visits, and she valued the time with him greatly. To her delight, he seemed to enjoy the time as well.

During their first year in the village Ms. Flood became pregnant. The couple looked forward to the birth of their child, but when the time came for Ms. Flood to give birth the delivery did not go well. A healthy baby girl was born, but sadly, Ms. Flood died during childbirth.

Mr. Flood was devastated. Not only had his dreams of reaching a village and establishing a church failed, but now his wife and ministry partner was deceased. He also had an infant daughter he believed he could not raise. So, Mr. Flood left the girl with another missionary couple from another village. The infant girl was in the care of the missionary couple, but the couple mysteriously died only weeks after receiving the infant. It was believed that the witch doctors poisoned them. The infant ended up with an American couple, the Byrds, who were short-term missionaries. They named the girl Agnes, and she became known as Aggie Byrd.

The Byrds loved Aggie and raised her in America. Yet, she learned the story of her life and often wondered why her life had been filled with so many tragedies. She also began asking serious questions about the meaning of her life and why her natural parents' ministry seemed so futile. Nonetheless, she was a person of faith, and while attending Bible college she met a minister, E V Hill, and married him.

Upon checking the mail one day she discovered a Swedish magazine there. She couldn't read the words, but she clearly recognized the name on a gravestone in one of the articles: Svea Flood. She took the magazine to a friend, who translated the article for her. It was the story of a young boy from Central Africa who sold eggs to a missionary wife. He told how she had shared Christ with him long ago and that it was because of her witness that he came to know the Lord, start a school, and soon after, lead most of the village to Christ. At the time of the article's publication, his witness had spread to more than six hundred nearby villages. Svea's faithful ministry to that small boy who came to sell her eggs had resulted in an incredible harvest of souls for the kingdom of God.

After reading the article Aggie told her husband that she had to try to find her father. They searched the city, and finally they found her dad. She went to a small bedroom and found her father—a man who had long ago left his faith. He was at the point of death. He became emotional and while weeping tried to apologize for leaving her with others. She assured him that she had been raised by great people and had a great life. The main point, she explained, was that he understand that he hadn't failed so many years ago in Africa. Because of his and Svea's ministry, hundreds of people were walking with the Lord. Aggie asked her father to rededicate his life to Jesus Christ, and the former missionary who had lost so much prayed with her to receive Jesus as Lord and Savior.

This story encouraged me that success for ministry was simply to reach a child and help shape the child's life. Success as an attorney could be building a home for someone without one.

Millard Fuller, who grew up poor in Alabama, became an attorney and successful in business. His faith led him to renewal and change. He and his wife sold everything they owned and began to try to live out the teachings of Jesus Christ. The result was coming up with an affordable house-building model that first worked in Zaire, Africa. However, the model was expanded to America as well. With the help of Linda Fuller, Habitat for Humanity was formed. This Christian organization has provided a program for moving families in need into new homes since 1976. Mr. Fuller died in 2009, but his love and sacrifice became his legacy.

While my story isn't as dramatic as either of these amazing life stories, nor have I sacrificed as much as the people in these stories, ordinary people just like me can impact their community in some way. I hope my story and the stories of others who have helped serve as yet more stories that will encourage you to serve others, particularly children and families in poverty.

CHAPTER 1

A TITANIC MOMENT

H AVE YOU EVER had one of those days or months—maybe even years—when things just weren't going the way you wanted? For me, December of 1997 was that time. While the Christmas holidays usually brought cheer to my heart, this season was different. I was struggling with the need for direction.

I was also hurting because my mother, Lena Martin, was battling breast cancer. She was diagnosed six years earlier and had been cancer-free for five years. For breast cancer, we were told, five years was a milestone for survivability. Her doctors told us that the odds of surviving increase exponentially after that period.

But my hero—this gentle giant and saint of a woman— had been rediagnosed six months after the five-year period expired. That was 1996; this was 1997. Our prayers had not been answered. She still suffered with metastatic breast cancer that had recurred in her liver and a rib close to her lungs. I wondered if this would be the last Christmas I would spend with my mom.

Not only did I need a miracle that Christmas season, but I also needed vocational direction. I had finished law school in May 1996, passed the Arkansas Bar Exam that August, and was hired by a Little Rock law firm in March 1997. But I had a desire and calling to be bivocational—to be a minister and a lawyer, if one could believe that a person could be wired that way. I know what you are probably thinking—"That sounds like a weird combination"—but actually there are many people who do both. My mentor, whom I had just finished serving for three years throughout law school, Marion A. Humphrey, served as an attorney and then as a circuit judge when I worked for him. At the same time he was pastor of Allison Presbyterian Church in Little Rock. One of the reasons he hired me was my interest in gaining a seminary degree after law school. He had received his theological training at Harvard Divinity School and then returned home to Arkansas to attend the University of Arkansas Law School in Fayetteville.

But I had left the security of my position with Judge Humphrey for a position as an attorney in private practice—a very challenging idea for me. Before leaving Judge Humphrey's office and after completing law school I enrolled in a Master of Arts in Christian Ministries program at the Assemblies of God Theological Seminary, gaining ten hours towards that degree. Now I was in private practice and had little time for seminary training, even the modular classes that lasted for a week with pre and post sessions. I had also become credentialed with the Arkansas District Council of the Assemblies of God in the meantime, becoming a certified minister. I was pleased but wondered if I would ever satisfy the calling to ministry I still felt so strongly.

Even while I was asking these questions I was scheduled to speak at a commencement class of a Christian school. I remember wrestling with the future on the drive to the graduation. I felt such peace as the Lord seemed to speak to my heart: "I can make you a greater minister while you are an attorney than I could have as a seminary student. I can do anything!" The speech went well, and I felt very good about the possibilities, although there was nothing rational about this hope. I just knew that God was in control of my destiny—of my mother's health and of my future as well.

While uncertainties lingered, the self-doubt and worry over my mother seemed to culminate in a moment of insight on December 23, 1997. Earlier that day I had represented a woman whose two children had been removed from her by the state social services, Arkansas' Department of Human Services. My wife, Dawn, and I had agreed to go to a movie when I got out of court, but court lasted until 6:30, and the movie began at 7:00. The hearing was depressing. We made little headway in her review hearing on this date, and I wondered why we would have a hearing so close to Christmas; it certainly did not put me in the Christmas spirit.

Nonetheless, I was sure my planned diversion for the evening would. I love history, and I was going to watch a movie based on a true, historical event—the sinking of the *Titanic*. I really wanted to see the movie because of the historical aspect and also because I heard that, at that time, it was one of the most expensive movies that had ever been made. I was excited. I was disappointed that I didn't have time to go home and put on some blue jeans and get out of my suit. I would also have enjoyed eating dinner, but I knew I could have a hot dog and popcorn at the movie. I met Dawn and her mom and dad, Bob and Fran, and her brother and his wife, Joe and Glenda, at the ticket counter. We went into the Lakewood Movie Theater in North Little Rock. I was ready to lose my cares in the silver screen.

Now, both my family and I are pretty picky about the movies we see. I grew up in a strict Pentecostal church and home. I wasn't even supposed to go to movies, although my mom always let me go to preapproved movies. I taught the college and career Sunday school class at First Assembly of God in North Little Rock and always told my students that going to R-rated movies was just simply wrong. I had made the commitment not to go to those movies long ago—with a little encouragement from my mom.

More difficult was the new category of PG-13. I was clearly older than thirteen, but sometimes that rating could be a tip-off that some stuff I didn't need to see or hear could be in that movie. Although *Titanic* was PG-13, the information about the movie indicated that it was probably a movie I could see; in other words, not very much language, and obviously, no nudity or sex scenes.

Well, my information was wrong on both accounts. Shortly into the movie one of the characters used an offensive term that took the Lord's name in vain. I knew I might be in for a long evening. Here I needed some diversion worse than I had needed it in a long time— just a few moments of escape, please—and instead I found myself in a movie that was making me angrier by the minute. The reason was simple. I loved the movie—loved the music, the drama, the dialogue, the storyline, and the relationship between the heroine and the protagonist and antagonist. I also liked the historical aspect. Then it happened. The heroine undressed from the top up. I couldn't believe it. I asked Dawn, "Is this something a thirteen year old should be watching?" She told me what she often told me: "We bought the ticket. Just sit here and close your eyes." But I couldn't. I told her I would wait for her and her family outside.

I went outside feeling pretty moral and smug about it too. I remember thinking about how our nation compared to the *Titanic*—"the ship that even God couldn't sink," as one person said about the real ship. I thought about how the moral and cultural fiber of our nation had been adrift for some time, how we were cruising through deep, cold waters, very capable of hitting an iceberg. While I was thinking through these high and grandiose thoughts it began to rain. It had been a dreary day all day with light rain, but now the heavens opened, and it really started to rain—cats and dogs, as they say.

At that time I noticed something strange. I was propped up against the wall near the movie entrance seeking shelter from the rain by a large overhang connected to the theater roof. I saw an African-American woman pass by me with a little toddler behind her. He couldn't have been older than two and a half or maybe three years old. What was odd was that she did not have his hand, nor was she covering him with the umbrella she was holding. When they crossed in front of me and left the overhang she sped up—obviously, because the rain was coming down. But the child behind her was falling farther and farther behind.

I started thinking, "Should I get involved? What will she think about this white guy trying to get involved? Will she think I'm trying to abduct the child?" But while the woman had gotten to the parking lot and was running to a car, the child was getting closer and closer to the busy entryway to the theater. I knew I had to get involved. I ran—in my suit, without an umbrella—into the pouring rain. I reached the child before he got to the entryway by seconds, picked him up, and saw the vehicle the woman I assumed was his mother had gotten into. When I got to her car I beat on her window. She opened the window and said, "Where did he come from?" I told her what happened.

She said, "Boy, you were supposed to be with your mother." She was the boy's aunt. She had been oblivious to the fact that he was behind her.

Again, I felt pretty good about myself. I had intervened and, who knows, maybe saved the boy's life, I thought smugly. I was wet. My suit and shirt were clinging to me. But in that instant God interrupted the silence in my life. He spoke to my heart with clear direction. He shared with me that He was sending me to a group of people in danger just as the boy had been in danger. He said that I would have to get personally involved and that I would get messy, just as my suit and hair had gotten messy by the rain. I made it back to the overhang no longer so smug. In the midst of seeking a diversion God had given me my assignment.

Like Abram of old, I didn't get much in the way of details that night. God told Abram to pack up and start walking, and later He would tell him where he was going. (See Genesis 12:1.)

I wonder if Abram, later Father Abraham, had been wandering around like me. I wonder if he was questioning his current situation and wondering how he could impact his community in a special way. Then, in a flash, God showed up and spoke:

> Now the LORD had said unto Abram, Get thee out of thy country, and from thy kindred, and from thy father's house, unto a land that I will shew thee: And I will make of thee a great nation, and I will bless thee, and make thy name great; and thou shalt be a blessing: And I will bless them that bless thee, and curse him that curseth thee: and in thee shall all families of the earth be blessed. So Abram departed.
>
> —GENESIS 12:1–4

What caused God to show up with such promises? What did Abram think? All we know is what Abram did: He obeyed. But if Abram recognized that he had heard from God any clearer than me that night, I wouldn't believe it. Stunned and ready for God to work in my life in a fresh, new way, I saw my family exiting the theater. It had not been the *Titanic* experience I had wanted or expected, but it was a titanic moment in my life nonetheless.

Maybe you need a titanic moment. I really don't define my moment as an epiphany. I think God is always ready at any instance to capture our attention if we will just get still long enough to hear Him. We live in a noisy world, so sometimes we have to get alone, disappointed—even desperate—to hear from Him. If God would speak to me I know He will speak to you. My prayer in writing this book is that you will get still before the God who will make your calling crystal clear. Our generous God has a plan for your life and a specific way He wants you to touch your community. Why don't we pray right now:

> *Dear God, thank You for loving us. Thank You for speaking to us, especially in ways for which we are not prepared. Help us to hear Your voice and to move forward with Your great plan for our lives. In Jesus' name. Amen.*

CHAPTER 2

FRIED CATFISH
AT LASSIS INN

IMAGINE BEING SCHEDULED to get married in a month, being unemployed, and having few prospects for employment. I found myself in this very situation following my first year of law school. We had to agree not to work for our first year of law school as full-time students where I attended.

With the summer coming up I sent out one hundred letters for employment with law firms and judges. From those letters I got three interviews.

My fiancée, Dawn, was finishing her second year of medical school, and she and I were both living on student loans. My mom, Lena, was even more concerned than me. It was early May, and her only child was scheduled to be married on June 25. On a Sunday night she resorted to prayer. She went to the altar in the little church I grew up in and prayed that I would get a job.

That night when she got home Judge Marion Humphrey called her. "Please send your son to my office tomorrow. I have a job opening." This was an immediate, specific answer to prayer. She rejoiced.

I still remember walking into the tiny offices of the Pulaski County Circuit Court, First Division. The county courthouse was being renovated, and the court was stuck in the KARK-TV building on Third Street.

I opened the door to the office and met Annette, the judge's secretary at that time, and later a probation officer, as well as Linda, his case coordinator. They were kind to me. I was nervous and ready to get the interview completed. Leon, Judge Humphrey's law clerk, called for me and would be interviewing me for the job. The job was one I had never heard of—a pre-sentence officer. All I knew was I needed a job, and this was a job! There was even a salary! However, the job would be temporary, just for the summer.

Leon and I hit it off immediately. He was kind-hearted, and there was ease in our conversation. He was hungry for breakfast, so we walked across the street and continued the interview at the restaurant across the way. Leon put grape jelly on a sausage, egg, and cheese biscuit. I had never tried that combination but have to confess I loved it! After an interesting breakfast and wonderful interview, Leon told me he would recommend to Judge Humphrey that he hire me.

I was eager to meet Judge Humphrey. I walked into his tiny, temporary office, and he immediately impressed me as a kind man. He was warm and gracious to me. He told me that I was hired and that I could start the following Monday.

May 11, 1994, was a good day in my life. I began to meet the cast of characters in the drama that was First Division Circuit Court. I met Henry, Judge Humphrey's bailiff; Curtis, chief probation officer; Dwight, probation and pre-sentence officer; Tjuana, probation and pre-sentence officer and part-time law student; and Raymia, the judge's court reporter. The interesting thing was that Raymia and I were the only two Caucasians in the office among the nine staff members. Being the minority was truly eye-opening.

Sometimes being the minority was also uncomfortable. Over and over again as a pre-sentence officer I was called on to make sentencing recommendations for people awaiting a sentencing hearing. The problem became obvious: a disproportionate number of the pre-sentence reports I prepared were for young African-American males. I watched as they pleaded guilty or were found guilty by the jury or judge, and then it was up to me to suggest a sentence.

While I had assistance with standards for sentencing, suggesting sentences was difficult. I often wondered if there was any hope for the plight of these young men. I also wondered if some of them could have been spared probation, probation revocations, and the penitentiary if someone—anyone—had gotten involved in their lives before they began making the wrong decisions.

As a pre-sentence officer I had to gain information about their backgrounds. Over and over again the story was the same: These guys were being raised by a single mother or grandmother, dropped out or were kicked out of high school, and were living in poverty.

I became very broken over these guys. I felt God getting my attention to make a difference in the lives of some kids who were at risk to end up as the guys I was seeing every day. I knew the target—kids trapped in poverty, being raised by single moms, and who may be struggling with schoolwork.

Well, the summer quickly came to an end. Dawn and I were married, and Judge Humphrey, Linda, and Annette all came to the wedding. I was so pleased. When we returned from our honeymoon Leon told me that the judge felt like I was doing a good job. If I wanted to stay past the summer I could keep my job. I was so happy. The problem was, How could I go to school full-time and work for Judge Humphrey full-time? The answer: very carefully. The Judge allowed me to go to classes, leave work, and come back. I would come in early and stay late to get in my hours. As you can imagine this schedule meant that I would be working long hours, both at work and at school. The income, though, and the great relationships, not only from the Judge's staff but also among the legal community, were worth the sacrifice.

Since Dawn was in medical school studying to be a pediatrician she didn't miss me much. I would get to work at 6:30 a.m. and leave law school at about 8:00 p.m. many evenings. I was also singing in choir at church and leading the college and career ministry. I was very busy, and time seemed to be flying as well.

Before I knew it I was done with law school, had passed the bar, and again needed a job. But in

November 1996 Curtis helped me see exactly where God was assigning me.

Curtis and Paul, a probation officer for another judge, always raved about how good the fried catfish was at this little restaurant in South Little Rock called Lassis Inn. They told me, "Jay, if you like fried catfish, you've gotta go to Lassis Inn!" So, on a particularly slow day at First Division, Curtis and I loaded up in his car and headed across town to Lassis Inn. Paul was going to meet us there.

I thought the name was interesting. To me, it sounded more like a place you would spend the night instead of eat. But what I found out was that Lassis Inn was kind of a neighborhood hangout. They sold beer in brown bags, had a jukebox with Motown music (which I love), and the patrons of the establishment were interesting. Being a white guy who grew up in the country, I was pleased that Curtis and Paul had their side arms.

We ordered catfish, sat down, and waited. I seemed out of place there. I was the only white guy and, besides Curtis and Paul, was the only guy not smoking or drinking. Some guys were in booths with their significant others getting an early start to their Friday night date.

The catfish came, and Curtis and Paul were correct; if you want to eat good catfish, go to Lassis Inn. It was a wonderful, traditional fried catfish dinner with all the trimmings, including sweet tea that was sweet enough to give you a headache.

Curtis and I told Paul good-bye and headed back down 28th Street. I asked Curtis where we were going, and he told me he knew a short-cut back to work. The next thing I knew we were driving through homes that looked like army barracks. They were identical, with blue, green, or yellow siding. I could see a playground in the distance.

"Who lives here?" I asked.

"Jay, this is the projects—government housing," Curtis responded. I later found out that we had driven by the Amelia B. Ives Housing Project off Roosevelt Road in Little Rock.

From that day on I knew I had found a place where kids probably lived who were poor, who were being raised by single moms, and who were at risk to become the people for whom I prepared pre-sentence reports. I knew I had found my target.

To his credit, and upon my request, Curtis returned me to the projects. We drove around, and on the backside of the projects in a row of houses with orange brick down a narrow street called Ives Walk I saw two boys and a girl playing basketball. The scene was quite depressing. The basketball goal was just in the ground, with no concrete upon which to bounce a basketball. Instead, a dirt circle was there where the concrete was supposed to go, with a mud puddle in the middle of the "court." The goal was high, and the rim had no net.

"Curtis, I have to get out and play basketball with those kids."

"Be careful, Jay. I'll get out with you," Curtis said.

That day I met two brothers and a sister being raised by a single mom. I asked one of the brothers if they went to church, and he said that they did not. I told him that soon I would bring church to them.

Curiously, I could see some adults, including young men on the porch of a home in the distance, but no one came up or in any way thought it was odd that some white guy would get out and start playing with the kids. I was also shocked at how open the kids were to talk to me and to hang out with me.

As we left Curtis told me that he didn't want to concern me, but two of the guys on the porch in the distance had handguns. "This is a dangerous place, Jay. You need to know that," he said.

But I was hooked. I had met some kids—some kids who weren't involved in church. They were definitely part of my target audience, and I knew that I had to reach them.

––––––––––––

Have you ever wondered how Abram knew he was where he was supposed to go? How did he know he was at the place God had sent him? God had not provided a map to the land. God had not described it to him either. Instead, after some difficulties in Egypt, Genesis 13 tells us that Abram let his nephew Lot pick the land he wanted to own and where he wanted to graze his cattle. Abram took the second choice and ended up in Canaan. It did not have the glamour of the luscious plain near Sodom and Gomorrah that Lot picked, but it was right for Abram. I just think Abram fit in the land he was called to like a hand fits in a glove. He knew it was a match.

Aren't you glad that God has place-assignments for us? Where is your place? Has God called you to your street or block? Maybe the place you fit is your office, and it is your Ives Walk. Maybe it is the class you teach or the co-workers you encourage. Maybe it is neighborhoods like Ives Walk, where children survive instead of thrive. Wherever that place is, give the people there 100 percent and know that God has a purpose for your place-destination.

CHAPTER 3

THOUGH NONE
GO WITH ME

T HE DAY CAME when I knew I had to go to Ives Walk and do something, even if I didn't have all the answers. While I knew I had to go there, I had some loose ends to tie up. First, I was leading the college and career ministry at First Assembly.

A few months earlier my passion for the children in the inner city led me to share a lesson on being outwardly focused. I asked the students what I hoped would serve as probing questions: "Tonight, if you go home and you have no trouble sleeping, but across town kids can't go to sleep because of gunfire in the night, does that bother you?" I asked, "If after church tonight you go to a restaurant, eat, and hang out with friends, but all across our city children will go to bed hungry, does it matter to you?" I then challenged them, "Are we responsible for those kids? Could they count on us to get involved?"

I am not sure whether my words impacted those students, but about six months later I was having trouble sleeping in my safe neighborhood and eating my abundance of food. God had gotten my attention so thoroughly about kids that I could hardly see a little kid dressed poorly without crying. I said, "Lord, what can I do?" I would drive around Little Rock in some of the more challenged neighborhoods praying for God to speak to me further about this developing passion within me.

I had a cousin who shared my passion for lost, desperate, and at-risk kids. Over several meals we enjoyed visiting about starting a ministry in Little Rock to reach students. When I finally made up my mind that the neighborhood to reach was Ives Walk I visited with my cousin about moving from theory (reaching kids) to practice, actually getting a date to go to Ives Walk.

I'll never forget a meeting at Shoney's Restaurant in Benton over a huge breakfast buffet. It was early November 1997, and I knew I had to act. I wondered if my cousin would join me. At that meeting my cousin raised a number of reasons why we should wait. Winter was coming, we needed to pray more, and we had no clear idea of what we were supposed to do. In addition, if we waited we could recruit volunteers to go with us. His words made sense. I left that meeting knowing I had made the right "head" decision but not the right "heart" decision. However, he was my only other potential partner in this ministry, and I didn't want to get started without him. And, what he said made sense.

Then in December I had my titanic moment. After that event I knew I was willing to go alone. And I did. Now, instead of driving around Little Rock I would drive around South Little Rock and make swings through Ives Walk.

It was winter, and there wasn't much activity. But spring was on the way. My cousin and I decided on March 15, 1998, to go to a coffee house together in Hot Springs. "Coffee house" is probably too formal of a name for this place; it was basically an oversized garage at some folks' house. They loved to sing and would invite people over to sing, eat, and listen to a message. This was the night I had waited on. I knew that the next day, rain or shine, kids out or not, cousin with me or not, I was headed to Ives Walk to begin something. God would show me what to start.

I still remember the dear brother leading that service. That night they gathered around me. My cousin told them what I was going to do the next day. He couldn't go with me, so I would be going all alone. Somehow I knew I would start alone. They prayed God's anointing and protection over me. I left that service knowing I was ready to begin.

Maybe you have been waiting to be obedient because no one shares your passion for the group or ministry to which God has called you. I realized something gradually during this time of my life: Every great work of God, every great move of God where He reveals Himself to humanity in a greater way, occurs because someone—and sometimes only one person—was willing to be used.

Many people in the Bible had to go alone. David must have felt alone when he went out against Goliath by himself. I often wonder how it must have felt to be a kid and to watch warriors let you go out alone to fight the giant, with no one to go with you. David walked out, trusting in God's provisions and protection, and he swung the rock from a sling that knocked a giant down. (See 1 Samuel 17.)

I believed the problems facing these kids were larger than the problem Goliath posed to the Israeli army; yet, with God's help, the giants of poverty, sin, and need could be destroyed.

Abram must also have felt alone. He had Sarai and Lot, his nephew, and some servants, but he was leaving every other family relationship behind. Genesis 12:4–5 (NIV) tells the story:

> So Abram went, as the Lord had told him; and Lot went with him. Abram was seventy-five years old when he set out from Harran. He took his wife Sarai, his nephew Lot, all the possessions they had accumulated and the people they had acquired in Harran, and they set out for the land of Canaan, and they arrived there.

Here we find no debate or argument by Abram— just simple obedience. God said to go, and rather than holding on to Harran, Abram goes.

Most people who dream of making a difference in the lives of others have to wonder at some point if they have what it takes. Over and over again in this season I found myself questioning, Would it be presumptuous for me to go alone? Then the words to this old song came to mind, and I was reminded all over again that as Christ-followers we are never alone!

Though none go with me
I still will follow
Though none go with me
I still will follow
Though none go with me
I still will follow
No turning back
No turning back

My prayer for you is that you will go or you will begin or you will take that first step. You will probably have to do it alone. Do it anyway!

And when we do it anyway, it is at that point that we realize that we are not alone. God is with us. "This is the way," God says, "walk in it." (See Isaiah 30:21.)

CHAPTER 4

SATURDAY AFTERNOONS IN THE HOOD

SATURDAY, MARCH 16, rolled around. The sun was shining, I knew where I was headed, and I was afraid. I had set my expectations pretty low that day; I would walk out on the basketball court and maybe meet a kid or two, play a little basketball, not get shot, and call the day a complete success.

I turned my truck off Roosevelt, down Main Street, and then turned onto Twenty-Ninth Street. The basketball court was to the side of a grassy field at the corner of Twenty-Ninth and Cumberland.

I parked my truck near some houses on Twenty-Ninth Street, not too far from the court, and willed myself to get out. I knew the neighborhood was dangerous, but I also knew God had called me there. I remember feeling afraid. My young wife, Dawn, was at home, and I really didn't want to die on this day. I said a prayer that the Lord would keep me safe and that He would please let me meet at least one kid.

I had absolutely no plan. I had nothing with me either. One would think since I was going to a basketball court I would have at least brought a basketball, but I did not.

As I approached the court I could see the houses pretty well. No one was stirring. I was afraid I had come too early, although it was after noon. I walked to the court and stood there. The court was crude—two basketball goals with no nets and a slab of concrete with graffiti sprayed on the court.

I stood there for what seemed an eternity trying to decide if I should just pray again and leave. I had to look as out of place as I felt. "What a great plan," I thought. "Stand out here in the middle of the projects! That's a great plan!"

Then out of the corner of my eye I could see a boy heading toward me. He had a basketball wedged between his hip and his right arm. He treated me as though it was not strange at all to see a random white guy standing on his basketball court. He was very open—so open, in fact, I later worried about him around strangers.

He was nine years old, and his name was Ezekiel.[1] He was also a pretty good basketball player. We talked, and I told him to tell his friends that I would be coming out every Saturday at noon to hang out, play basketball, and to tell them about Jesus. I told him I would bring my Bible and tell them Bible stories also.

After explaining my plan to him, he said he thought that was cool. He assured me he would tell his friends, and the next week maybe more folks would come out.

---

1 This name has been changed.

Looking back, Ezekiel was the perfect kid for that day—so open and so nice to me.

While I went out alone, I wouldn't have traded it for anything now. I was vulnerable in a way I would have never been with a team. Ezekiel accepted me, and honestly, probably felt a little sorry for me.

I kept my promise to Ezekiel and came back the next Saturday at noon. On this day there were kids everywhere. I met three young men I would mentor—Nick and Randy, and Montez. I met a bunch of other kids, and with few exceptions they shared these common characteristics: they were young, had more than one sibling, were being raised by a single mother, were in need of better clothing and shoes, and were hungry. But the thing that gripped me more than anything else was their desire for love and attention from me. Each child opened up to me, sharing their story, wanting to hug me, feel my "white guy" hair, wanting me to carry them, pick them up to help them get closer to the basketball goal, and share their lives. I was amazed.

As a matter of fact, I just kept showing up on Saturdays. We had a good thing going. Each Saturday, regardless of the weather or my personal agenda, I just showed up.

The hard work, though, as it is for any new group, was learning names, trying to remember brother and sister connections, and learning where in the neighborhood the kids lived. This occurred rapidly though.

Typically we would play basketball, I would set my Bible at the edge of the court, and when we were done I would gather them around me on the grassy field. I would then read the Bible, talk with them about spiritual things, and pray with them. Then we would cross Twenty-Ninth Street and walk over to a little neighborhood store, Barnes Store, and buy frozen ICEEs or soda pops. Always before I left I would tell them that I loved them.

I never thought that a basketball court and a grassy field could become a sanctuary where God could touch hearts and lives, but that is exactly what happened. One heart that was being touched was my heart. I received such a sense of how Jesus was loving children through me. When I touched them, He touched them; as I loved them, He loved them through me. Connections were easy and rapid.

I learned a lesson Moses must have learned. In Exodus we read the story of how Moses left his home and status as a prince in Egypt for the Desert of Midian. After murdering an Egyptian in his fevered desire to help his fellow Hebrews, he was a fugitive. He met a priest named Jethro in the desert, married Jethro's daughter, and began watching his herds. One day while in the desert with the sheep, God showed up. God's presence burned with brightness in the form of a bush that was on fire. The bush captured Moses' attention, and then God captured Moses' attention. On that desert floor Moses was ordered to remove his shoes because he was on holy ground.

It occurred to me one day that the basketball court was holy ground. Playing basketball with children was becoming an act of worship. I realized God wants to set His people on fire, just like that bush. He wants to set our hearts aflame by the Holy Spirit to burn but not burn up.

As a matter of fact, I have come to believe that this is Jesus' will for all of us. When I was a child sometimes my parents would follow the siren sound of a fire truck. We were curious to see what was on fire. Fires always create curiosity. I believe Jesus wants to set us ablaze with the love and glory of the Holy Spirit. Some out of curiosity and others to escape the cold world will be attracted to the light and heat of our passion's fire.

As the spring turned into summer the boys and I felt like we were on fire. To say it is hot during Arkansas summers at noon on concrete without any shade is to recklessly dabble in foolish understatement. Even Barnes Store ICEEs couldn't put out the heat of our summer meetings.

While it was hot, it also became something like sacred. One day after our game I noticed my Bible lying on the corner of the basketball court. Only God could turn a graffiti-ridden slab of concrete used as a basketball court into a sanctuary. Only God could connect the hearts of inner-city kids with a lawyer–minister who had little to offer other than love. Only God could use the Bible and a basketball to accomplish His purposes for a fatherless generation of at risk kids.

Had I come with only a Bible or a church invitation I might not have gotten involved into the kids' lives. Had I come with only a basketball—if I had one in the first place—I might could have started a youth basketball league. There is nothing wrong with either approach. But somehow the marriage of the Bible and the basketball unlocked miracles.

One thing I didn't have out there, though, was my briefcase. I had to leave the trappings of my day job behind. These kids didn't need a lawyer; they needed a friend. But as they learned I was a lawyer they didn't tell me legal jokes. Lawyers were very respected in their neighborhood, but a lawyer/minister? That was an interesting combination!

It wasn't about an inanimate object—Bible, briefcase, or basketball—yet the way God uses common things in His hands is truly amazing.

God asked Moses what he had in his hand. (See Exodus 4:2.) God took Moses' staff—just his common, ordinary, everyday tool of the sheep-herding trade—and used it to perform miracle after miracle.

What is in your hand? Does it seem pretty ordinary? If we take the common, ordinary, everyday tools and objects of our lives and give them to the Lord, He will consecrate them. He will use them in ways we never dreamed.

What are you waiting for? If you have a paintbrush paint a masterpiece for Jesus or paint some widow's home. If you have some money use some of it to make someone's life better. If you have some time on your hands invest it in a mentoring program in your community. We all have resources, which, if dedicated to God and channeled appropriately, can become a miracle. I know you have a Bible and a basketball in your future.

CHAPTER 5

CAMP LOVE 1998

THERE ARE OBVIOUSLY different levels of poverty. I grew up relatively poor by most standards. My mom and dad were on food stamps when I was born, and when I was two years old my dad was placed in an institution due to mental illness. So, money was tight. But I was loved, and my mother sacrificed to make sure I had things.

In Ives Walk I continued to be overwhelmed by the physical needs of the children. One event early on involved one of the young men whom I would mentor for many years: Glen. No child caught my attention like this kid did. He was so shy he would never make eye contact with me. His clothes were old and worn out (and that was not the style then). One day in April he looked up at me and said, "Today's my birthday."

I said, "Great. When's your party? What are you getting for your birthday?"

"Nothing," he said very sadly.

His answer immediately revealed to me my stupidity for asking those questions. His answer also gripped my heart. My mom always acknowledged my birthday.

I always got some kind of gift. But Glen was the sixth of eight brothers living with a single mother who was working two jobs to try to pay the bills. Balloons, ice cream cake, party hats, and birthday gifts just weren't in the budget eight times during the year.

I tried to make up for my stupid question. I went out to my truck and got out an old basketball. I handed it to him and said, "Happy birthday, Glen!" His face lit up—and he never left my side again. That simple act broke through to a part of Glen that I am not certain I could have reached any other way.

This boy helped open my eyes to a greater degree to see the poverty and needs in the neighborhood. I also committed to mentor him and his two younger brothers. I began taking them to church with me on Sundays, celebrating birthdays and Christmases with them (including a birthday cake, a dinner, always a present for birthdays and a gift for Christmas, and usually a movie, which was never rated anything more than PG), and hanging out with them every chance I could get. I mentored these young men for ten years. They are like sons to me, even though I seldom see them today.

Even though my desire to reach out to this neighborhood and mentor a couple of children was happening, I was overwhelmed by the physical needs and poverty I saw and the number of kids in the neighborhood with the needs.

I also found that many parents, mostly single mothers, were forced to work long hours or take care of young babies and that the children had a lot of discretionary time on their hands. With summer coming I knew this was not a good thing. It was as though they were waiting for something, but unfortunately not much was going on for the kids in the neighborhood.

I became very burdened for all the kids in the neighborhood. I knew I needed a plan or program to give the kids something to do but to also get more people involved to touch the kids and to meet the parents as well.

I dreamed of some kind of a camp. I wanted to take the kids out of the inner city, bring along some of their parents, recruit camp workers, and in registering kids and parents for the camp, get their names and addresses.

So, while a plan was starting to take place, I did what seemed to be the natural progression: I thought of some places that seemed to be fun, I went door to door to get permission forms signed, I recruited volunteers, and I designed a T-shirt. The camp would be for three consecutive Saturdays, and each Saturday we would do events outside the neighborhood.

First I contacted the Arkansas Game and Fish Commission. For some time I had wanted to take the kids fishing, but I thought taking them to a stocked pond owned and maintained by Game and Fish seemed like a great idea. The commission was very accommodating. They gave us free use of a stocked pond, offered to provide fishing poles, tackle, and everything needed for fishing. I was overwhelmed at the generosity.

We also called the Little Rock Zoo, who gave us a discount for the large group that would be attending.

Finally, I planned a cookout at Pinnacle Mountain State Park in Little Rock.

A team also developed—namely, my wife, Dawn; her parents, Bob and Fran; Curtis from Judge Humphrey's office; and a few other workers. I was pleased that a team was coming together.

One immediate need was transportation. I didn't know how many kids would sign up. I knew that if only a few signed up I could probably borrow a van from my church and drive them. But a huge number of kids signed up—like almost all the kids and their siblings who were coming to play basketball every Saturday. With that large number I knew I needed a bus and a CDL-qualified driver.

This need caused me to approach one of the pastors at First Assembly, Rod Loy. Pastor Rod had a heart for the inner city and was immediately struck by what I had been doing on my own. He said I could definitely have a bus, and he would give me a list of CDL-qualified bus drivers. Soon I had enough drivers for each of the three days.

The T-shirts came in, and the week before Camp Love I went door-to-door and handed out the T-shirts. I have never seen so much excitement over a T-shirt. The shirts were fairly cheap, a regular, white T-shirt with black lettering and design. But when I handed the shirts to the kids you would have thought that I handed them a one-hundred-dollar bill. For the last fifteen years I have seen the T-shirts still being worn by kids who have become adults. It truly impressed me; they were so thankful, and it was such a simple thing. The funny thing, though, is that I still have my T-shirt also.

I was experiencing such euphoria that I knew Camp Love would be cool—as long as we didn't have a student eaten by a tiger at the zoo or have a hook through a kid's nose while fishing.

Looking back now, I have to say we made a lot of mistakes with the first Camp Love. We had the camp in July—in the middle of the day. The time probably wasn't the best. Also, each event was outside. We went to the Little Rock Zoo for Day 1. Curtis came to me, and told me that he thought one of the students was getting too hot. One thing I had failed to do was plan on having drinks—even water—in the Arkansas summer midday heat. We were able to find some bottled water, get the kids hydrated, and I am happy to report that we didn't lose any. Unfortunately, they were working on the zoo and had some of the animal exhibits closed also.

I love the zoo, but I was really looking forward to Day 2. This would be the day we would go fishing. This day we were ready. We had sack lunches and plenty of water! The day had all the makings for a great one. The weather was warm but not too warm, we had a good crowd, including parents, and we had a great bus driver. Unfortunately, things went downhill from there. The location was difficult to find. We were in a huge school bus, and we had to turn around a couple of times. But we finally found the pond. It was not located in the middle of a pristine meadow, however, as I had envisioned. Instead, it looked a little bit like a cattle pond— very little grass, with rocks and dusty earth. But we were going to fish. I noticed in the distance some kind of a business that seemed to be operating also, but we were well away from them.

The kids loved fishing. My job was baiting hooks and visiting with kids and their parents while they fished.

Then it began. Shooting! I investigated in the direction of the shooting to discover that the business was a shooting target range. Imagine fishing in a war zone and you would have a picture of our fishing experience. I don't know if it was because the fishermen and women were nervous or the fish in the water could hear the shooting—or maybe there just weren't any fish in there—but only one of our students caught something that was a little bigger than a minnow. He insisted on taking the fish with him. Then I remembered what we had forgotten—something to take caught fish back in. Fortunately, it was not an issue. His mother convinced him that he would be the recipient of great ridicule if he came home with that fish.

Well, the day wasn't a total loss. The lunch was great, everyone had fun, and I think everyone knew that we were trying. That meant the world not only to the parents but also the students.

The final day, I have to admit, I was ready to close the camp out.

Again, the weather was sweltering, and we were outside at a park in the heat. We grilled hamburgers and hot dogs and played on playground equipment. We had fun, but the heat was horrid. We closed out the camp by riding back on the bus, singing songs, and feeling as though we had connected in a special way.

After analyzing the camp we made up our mind that if we could do it again we would do it very differently. No more outside activities in the heat of the day! Also, never again would I arm kids with a big stick with a sharp hook on the end of it. I would take kids fishing, but always in small groups and never en masse—and never again near a shooting range!

This is what I believe: Do something, even if you don't get it perfect! Sometimes I think we wait until everything is perfect until we take the next step. Taking the first step is difficult, but everything is new. It is tough to advance, but it is necessary.

Thank God His heroes of faith in the past just simply took the next step. Abram did more than begin a journey, but he did the hard work of passing through potentially deadly countries, settling his family in the plain, separating from his nephew, Lot, and doing the things necessary to fulfill God's plan.

Dr. George Wood, the general superintendent of the Assemblies of God, in a sermon at First Assembly told us about a song he sang often in his ministry. The first verse goes like this:

> Trod on, trod on, trod on, trod on
> Trod on, trod on trod on, trod on

He said, "There's also a chorus!"

> Trod on, trod on, trod on, trod on
> Trod on, trod on, trod on, trod on

The song also has a couple of verses. Can you guess them?

Sometimes, we just have to take the next step. We have to just "trod on!"

CHAPTER 6

CLOTHE MY CHILDREN

C AMP LOVE, ALTHOUGH a humble attempt, captured the hearts of the parents and students in a way that was shocking and hard to explain. I had many mothers tell me while usually fighting back tears that until we came nothing was happening for their kids. They were so happy that we were there, and it seemed that hope was being reestablished in many hearts.

After Camp Love we also had some information about the kids to distribute to potential mentors. One day after I took photographs of all of the kids who needed mentors, Dawn took large index cards and wrote their name and address on the cards.

For some time Dawn and I had given to a ministry that provided the photograph and basic information about a child in a developing country. We would send money, and he would write us letters. We would write back. The photographs of the children always moved us more than anything else.

We tried to apply this same principle to the kids in Ives Walk. I was also so pleased Dawn was willing to write the information on the index cards. My penmanship was terrible, but hers was excellent. The cards were obviously a humble attempt but looked very nice.

My mother was in the hospital more and more during the summer of 1998. Dawn and I spent a lot of time there with her. For a long day in the hospital after we took the pictures of the kids I pasted pictures, and Dawn wrote information. We were preparing for our meeting after a worship service at First Assembly when we would invite interested people to mentor some of these kids.

I was pleased at the response. We were able to secure several mentors for several kids and their siblings. Judge Humphrey also became a mentor, along with some of my relatives, including my Aunt Mary Voss. Scores of people from First Assembly began to faithfully mentor kids that summer.

No sooner had we signed up mentors and wrapped up Camp Love than we began to think and pray about the upcoming school year. One day I was jogging by the Arkansas River when God spoke to my heart. It was along this river trail that God often had spoken to me about this ministry. He never spoke in an audible voice, but He just confirmed my passion and heart for the people we were reaching.

"Clothe my children." The words God spoke to my mind on this particular run were so clear. I knew God was speaking to my heart. I began talking to God: "Lord, there's probably two hundred kids in the projects. How could I clothe them all?"

Again, "Clothe my children" came to my mind so clearly.

I realized my desire to do something for the kids before they went back to school was truly God's inspiration. So, I took the next—logical?—step. I thought, "If these kids are going to be clothed, what clothes do they need?" I got a legal pad and decided to go door-to-door and find out clothes needs and sizes. I made a list of clothing items—pants, shirts, socks, and underwear.

I was really out there now. In asking what clothes were needed I had implied that I would help with the need. I even told them I would help. The only problem was I had no idea how it would happen.

After a full two days gathering information I had several sheets of needs listed. The parents were overjoyed that they were going to have help with back-to-school clothes. I felt good about what I had done but also felt the need that existed in Ives Walk as I had never felt the need before.

I finished on a Saturday. I was back at St. Vincent Hospital spending time with my mother that evening. She was very ill, and my heart was breaking over her illness. I got a call from Dr. Garrison on my cell phone while there at the hospital. He told me he was preaching about love the next day at First Assembly, he had heard about my outreach to the Ives Neighborhood, and he wondered if I would share during his message about what I was doing. I was so shocked. In the midst of my sadness while visiting with my mom and my apprehension with biting off more than I could chew I knew God was at work to assist the people of Ives Walk with clothes. I also felt that God had remembered my mother and her illness. My faith was building.

The next day I stood in front of over a thousand people and shared with them what I had done. I will never forget what I said. Pastor Garrison introduced me, and I came down from the choir loft in my choir robe and joined Pastor Garrison on the platform. He then said, "Jay, take a couple of minutes to share what you are doing."

I said, "I don't know if I can tell you what I'm doing in a couple of minutes."

Pastor Garrison said, "Sure you can," and the crowd laughed heartily.

I did share in a couple of minutes, having never shared with a crowd that big. The people were moved, but Pastor Garrison said he wanted to take up an offering for the clothes. Miraculously, enough money was raised to buy everything on the list. The only thing we did not buy at that time was shoes. In Ives Walk shoes are important, and we could not get just any shoes.

Right before my eyes God came through. I stepped out on faith again, and He helped me. He met the overwhelming need.

The next matter was logistics. How do you purchase clothes for a couple of hundred kids with varying sizes, styles, etc.? We made vouchers, got busses and drivers, and took over Wal-Mart on a Saturday. Wal-Mart on Levy in North Little Rock, Arkansas, very kindly said that we could use their store. They set up a cash register just for us. We took a bunch of moms and kids with us to Wal-Mart, and they had a set amount of money to spend.

They were able to get not only clothes but also school supplies. We basically took over Wal-Mart, and I wish I had a photograph of the line waiting to check out. It was truly amazing.

During this time Henry Alyce Tucker, the director of the Keenagers, the senior adult ministries for First Assembly, approached me. She said that she had seen a show on the need for tennis shoes for inner-city kids. The show depicted kids whose feet were blistered and bleeding because they continued wearing shoes that were too small for their feet. She said that her group wanted to commit to providing a pair of shoes for each child in the Ives neighborhood.

I was amazed. God doesn't forget anything. The only thing we did not purchase at that Wal-Mart was shoes. Now we would be able to purchase cool tennis shoe for each child.

I talked to Nick, Glen, and Randy to find out what was cool. Frankly, I don't even remember the name brand then. We called a shoe store, and they agreed to sell us the shoes at a discount because of the volume. It was determined that during an outreach for Thanksgiving we would distribute the shoes the Keenagers had purchased.

My experience with God providing should not have surprised me. Over and over again in Scripture we see that God provided needs when people step out in faith.

So many times I am reminded of Jesus' admonition to His disciples in John 6. The crowds following Jesus were hungry. They were far from any town, and the hour was late. Jesus told His disciples to feed the people.

Immediately the disciples saw how great the need was and the lack of supply, but they found five loaves of barley bread and two fish from a boy who had brought his dinner. They brought the little they had to Jesus. Jesus blessed the meal and began to distribute a never-ending supply of food to the people. Baskets-full were taken up also from the leftovers. Amazing!

It is amazing to read that story. It is even more amazing when that story gets played out in our own lives. The resources show up at the point we step out in faith to meet the felt needs of others.

Abram had to have a moment where his faith was tested. After promising Abram all the land he could see in every direction God promised him a natural-born child would be his heir. This old man, with a wife who was well past the age of child-bearing, was given this promise: "And I will make thy seed as the dust of the earth: so that if a man can number the dust of the earth, then shall thy seed also be numbered" (Gen. 13:16).

Later, in Genesis 15, the Lord gave another promise to Abram: "And he brought him forth abroad, and said, Look now toward heaven, and tell the stars, if thou be able to number them: and he said unto him, So shall thy seed be" (v. 5).

The same thing will happen for you. Allow God to stretch your faith. Claim the promises in God's Word for yourself. Then take those promises and watch as God meets the needs of others through you. He will never let you down. You can count on Him to come through in dramatic fashion.

CHAPTER 7

GIVING THANKS
AT ST. JOHN

SUMMER TURNED INTO fall, and very quickly our minds turned to Thanksgiving. For me, this would be a special one. I had so much for which to give thanks. I was so pleased with the birth of this ministry!

The issue was we needed a place in the neighborhood to gather everyone to enjoy a Thanksgiving meal together. Through Judge Humphrey I had met the pastor of St. John Baptist Church, who graciously offered to let us use his church's fellowship hall to feed people during Thanksgiving week.

This would be the first event where First Assembly members would become introduced to the ministry, as we needed lots of workers to prepare food and to distribute the food as well. In addition, Henry Alyce Tucker determined that this would be the event to give out the tennis shoes.

The night finally arrived. Dr. Garrison and several ministers from First Assembly were present. Everyone was excited about having a Thanksgiving feast, but the kids were excited because they knew they had a new pair of shoes waiting on them.

Getting shoes for growing feet and then getting the kids that had signed up for the shoes at an event was a major logistical challenge. One lesson I learned was that the group of people who sign up for things are not always the people who show up at the event. We had a lot of kids who came to the feast who were not signed up for shoes. In addition, we had some kids who were signed up for shoes who were not present.

Faithful workers among the Keenagers ministry and our workers spent weeks after the event making shoe deliveries to kids who missed the event and getting shoes for the kids who were there who had not signed up for shoes.

As difficult as that was, I loved Dr. Garrison's observations from that night. In a message later that month Dr. Garrison said that it is difficult to keep up with the changing terms used by students. At the Thanksgiving event he heard kids saying over and over again as they tried on their shoes, "Man, these shoes are tight!" He thought there were problems with the way they fit. (And if some of the workers tried to get shoes on the kids who had not ordered them, they may not have fit.) But these kids were using the term *tight* to mean "really cool and trendy." Dr. Garrison realized what they meant and thought that was quite funny.

I was struck during the Thanksgiving event by a comment made by an observer of our ministry from one of the members of St. John who came to help. She said that it was obvious that a lot of love was being shown to her neighborhood to have the turnout that we had. I was so glad that someone from the religious community there in Ives Walk noticed that our motivation was love.

CHAPTER 8

CHRISTMAS

CHRISTMAS 1998 WAS very different from that season of the titanic moment in 1997. For me personally, I was dealing with the very real loss of my mother. This was the first Christmas since her death in August, and I knew Christmas would never be the same.

During the Christmas of 1997 I was so hopeful that my mother would get well. I also had the great joy of knowing God was calling me to something special; I just didn't know what it was. Even with ministry success, though, sometimes the idea of ministry is more intriguing than ministry itself.

Now, in December 1998, so much had been defined for me. I knew where God had called me, I had been embraced by God's miracle-working power, and my home church had embraced the ministry. Still, I have to confess I was feeling quite depressed.

Looking back, the ministry could have done more for Christmas. Dawn and I blessed the three boys we were mentoring. However, I could not shake the feeling that for the rest of my life my dear mom wasn't going to be around.

That is when it began happening. I began getting calls from people in the neighborhood who had needs. With every need that was identified, someone from First Assembly would step forward to meet the need. Sometimes it was for food. Other times it was help with some Christmas toys or even heating bills.

I remember getting lost in the neighborhood on Christmas Day. I had a turkey to hand off, and I couldn't find the person who was supposed to pick it up. They were late, and I was frustrated. Didn't they know this was Christmas Day? Didn't they know I was dealing with the loss of my mom? Didn't they know that at least Christmas Day should be a private, family day?

Then it dawned on me so clearly. For the rest of my life I would not hold any day sacred to me; I would abandon any and every day to minister to these precious people. As I made some more stops where I distributed gifts to kids that day, for some reason my mind fell on St. Nicklaus. While I certainly could not pass for Santa Claus, in that moment Christmas became something different to me. It was no longer a day to indulge my desires for gifts and free time. It was not a season to watch movies and hang out with family! No, it was another opportunity to minister to people who were hurting, hungry, and who were open to the story of Jesus' birth, death, and resurrection unlike any other time. With tears I repented of making Christmas a pagan holiday of indulgence. I promised myself that for as many years as the Lord would allow me to minister to Ives Walk, or wherever He should call me, I would use the Christmas holiday as one of the largest outreach opportunities of our ministry year.

———————————

Has the loss of a loved one caused you to be self-focused? Maybe it is the very real sense that your opportunity to make a difference has passed; that can seem like a death. I learned that as I focused on other people my sadness of spending my first Christmas without my mother diminished greatly. I was sad, yet my mind kept traveling back to the memories of seeing the smiling faces of adults and kids who expected nothing and yet got something. I challenge you to focus on someone else. It is the best way to overcome loss, and it may be the doorway to recovering your dream.

CHAPTER 9

SOUTH LITTLE ROCK COMMUNITY CENTER

W E STARTED 1999 knowing the year held lots of promise for our new ministry. The winter months were cold and snowy, and our Saturdays were interrupted by snow and ice.

One particularly snowy day I was so desperate to see my kids, and particularly because it was Nick's birthday I drove on the ice out to Ives Walk. My wife had sent me on an errand to the store for items to make chili. I thought I could just slide down to Ives Walk, which was only about six miles from my house, and slide back.

I learned an important lesson: Half-truths with one's wife, or anyone else, are the same as a full lie. I got to Ives Walk, and the guys were out playing in the snow. I saw Nick. I jumped out of the car, handed him a little gift, and we threw some snowballs. Somehow I got my doors locked, and my vehicle was running with the keys in the ignition.

There were lots of guys in the neighborhood who were certain they knew how to open locked car doors, but in the end they could not. So, I called Dawn and sheepishly admitted where I was. We had to contact her dad to get the spare key and drive from Jacksonville, nearly thirty miles away, to come get me the other key. I was very blessed to still have any gas in the vehicle by the time he came. It did, however, give me plenty of time to hang out with my kids.

As the snows of January and February began to melt and the weather warmed in March I realized we were nearing our one-year anniversary. We had learned the lesson of how effective having a building in the neighborhood could be to corral people and minister. So, my cousin and I began to dream again of having a service every week in Ives Walk.

I visited with the city of Little Rock about their community center. Apparently outside groups could use it free of charge for neighborhood enrichment programs. The city had become familiar with what we were doing, and we had the confidence particularly of the Little Rock Housing Authority.

So, in March, my cousin, Mark Farrow, and I had church on a Thursday night. On this night the South Little Rock Community Center (SLRCC) was not available, so we started our first night's service in a house owned by the Little Rock Housing Authority. My cousin led worship songs with his guitar, I preached, and then we served food. We attracted mostly the kids we had been reaching and prayed that we could also reach their parents.

As a matter of fact, as we dreamed about having a church service in Ives Walk, we hoped to target and reach the parents of the kids we were reaching. After all, their parents got them for so much more of their lives than we did. We wanted to impact their parents as well.

The next week, and then for the next two years, we would minister in the South Little Rock Community Center. Very soon others from First Assembly, some of the other people mentoring kids, and even curious city employees helped us. We would haul speakers and flowers and all kinds of things into the nondescript room. We tried to make it as inviting as possible. We never took it for granted even for one moment that the city was being generous. I kept reminding myself of this when we had to deal with leaky roofs and kids who had been suspended from the center's day activities not being allowed in for our services.

While it was not perfect, a church was born during these formative years. The SLRCC became a safe haven on Thursday nights for kids and also some adults who wanted to see their lives changed.

We fell into a pattern. I would take some kids with me, and we would begin knocking on doors and handing out flyers for the service about two hours before it began. I remember handing out some wild flyers. One said that the speaker for the night was a world-famous author whose book was the best-selling book of all times. Some people came out of curiosity, and of course I was talking about God and the Bible.

On one particular night I could see the extent of our effectiveness on the neighborhood. On Thursday nights one of the things we had to compete against was football practice. A couple of guys had formed a neighborhood team with some of our kids and were holding practice while we were trying to have church. We were gracious and knew that that football season was a temporary interruption.

However, during one of the practices one of the coaches, who had a son playing, got in a dispute with the son's mom and pulled a gun. All of a sudden our service was crashed with scared nine- and ten-year-old boys fleeing the chaos of an adult world. I cannot express to you how joyous it was to me that they ran to our service. They came to people who had proven to them that they cared and that, if necessary, would stand for them even in danger and chaos.

It was about this time that Nick, one of the boys I mentored, began to tell me an interesting thing every time I would leave him. He told me one day that if there were bad guys and they were going to shoot me, he would get shot so I wouldn't have to. In all my days I had never heard such a statement of love. He began telling me when I would leave: "I love you, and I would take a bullet for you, Jay!" I would leave weeping—tears of pain and joy!

CHAPTER 10

METRO WORSHIP CENTER

I LEARNED DURING MINISTERING to kids and families in the inner city that this kind of ministry attracted a lot of people with all kinds of different agendas. I tried to keep the agenda simple: We would love kids and share Jesus with them. We would love and get to know individual kids, even though more and more we resembled a traditional church. Well, it is hard to call it traditional; we met on Thursdays and made up our minds to never meet on Sundays.

As we began to dream of planting a church in Ives Walk we also studied the neighborhood. One day I was overwhelmed at the number of churches that surrounded the neighborhood. I counted twenty churches in a four-mile radius. I knew that we could never simply become another church competing for people to attend church on Sundays and Wednesdays. Our goal was to reach the truly unchurched and maybe bring them to a service in a setting that wasn't intimidating like a regular church. Then as they gave their lives to Jesus and we began to disciple them they could attend their neighborhood church on Sundays and Wednesdays.

I also began to prepare myself. I studied more and also began to get the credentials with my denomination, the Assemblies of God, that I should have been working on for some time. The Assemblies of God has three ministry levels, and the first is the certified minister's level.

I remember going to our state's district offices to get these credentials. At that meeting I saw a young man who I had taught in Sunday school and who had been away at Bible school. He was getting his credentials at the same time. He asked me what my ministry goal was. I told him to plant churches. He laughed and said, "You better get ready to move out west! In Arkansas there are already too many Assemblies of God churches." I smiled politely but knew that my calling was to plant a church in Arkansas—but one that wouldn't be like the church he envisioned.

It turned out that as Dr. Garrison became the district superintendent for our denomination and had to resign as pastor to lead in this new way, his executive pastor, Rod Loy, became senior pastor. The Lord had been speaking to Pastor Rod about church planting. There was excitement to attempt the first plant. It would be in or near Ives Walk.

First, however, we had to deal with a blessing that became a problem. In 2000 we were offered, free of charge, a warehouse that had several thousand feet of space. I was initially excited. The location was not the best. It was not in Ives Walk and was actually on the other side of the freeway. This guaranteed that whatever we did we would have to bus kids and families out of their neighborhood and into a new neighborhood. It was close but certainly inconvenient.

As soon as some of the folks got wind that we had been offered a building, all those people with wacky agendas came out of the woodwork. I had meetings with all kinds of people with all kinds of agendas for the building. I had never realized what a building would mean for some people. I was never oriented toward a building; I believed that buildings and other resources of that nature would follow our effectiveness in using what we had and growing relationships.

I was given a key to the warehouse, and one Sunday morning after dropping Nick, Glen, and Randy back off at their house after taking them to church I walked in the warehouse. I tried to envision what a church service would look like in that building. I became excited and tried to let the Lord stretch me. Standing in the front of a huge warehouse the Lord asked me what I saw. I saw an old warehouse that needed lots of work, that had a sagging roof and lots of problems. Yet, as I stretched my faith I could see people in my mind's eye. I saw a lot of dark, expectant faces. Then I felt compelled to preach my first sermon in our own building. So, I preached a sermon, took an offering, gave in the offering, sang some songs, gave an altar call, responded, and felt pretty foolish. But I was also obedient.

The Lord used that moment as a watershed moment. I believed at that moment that the Lord would use that facility as a church. It didn't make sense where it was located, but He could do it. He can do anything.

Then the entire offering of the warehouse became clear. I had to have something to give up—to give back to the God who had given it to me. Pastor Rod and I visited, and we believed that accepting the gift would forever get us on the wrong side of Interstate 30.

One day Pastor Rod and I drove around Ives Walk. We found a couple of vacant lots and began praying about those areas. I put on my attorney hat and worked with an abstract company. Soon we found something very hard to find in the inner city—someone who owned good title to a piece of property. It turned out to be a pawnshop, but the proprietor told us that he would donate the lot as long as we would also accept a smaller lot on the backside of the lot he was offering. He wanted a tax advantage and wanted to get rid of his holdings there. We graciously accepted.

Next we had to raise money to build a building. This would be a new building tailored for the needs we had rather than trying to use an old warehouse not tailored for our needs. The best thing was that this building would be built across the street from Ives Walk and only fifty yards from the house of the boys I was mentoring. This was the right spot and so much better than the warehouse, which was four miles away.

The day came, and Pastor Rod shared the need. He also shared that the Lord had laid it on his heart to plant churches. It was exactly what the Lord had been speaking to me. On that day a large enough offering was given to build the building of which we had dreamed. Just like when we had a need for clothes and shoes, the Lord came through. The facility would be fully funded.

While we became very excited, we still had to get our plans through the Little Rock Planning Commission. This board had become notorious for rejecting commercial ventures in residential neighborhoods. We knew we had our work cut out for us. Two builders attending First Assembly, Bill Darby and Randy Wright, assisted in amazing ways. They shepherded us through the process, and I put all the necessary notices out on the property. I served as the attorney for the project, and all of us volunteered our time. It was truly miraculous.

The board initially rejected our plans. We were saddened but scheduled the next board meeting to present again. This time we were aided by a blizzard. The board was trying to end their session but wanted to get finished with their agenda. No one was interested in asking hard questions, and our project was approved without all the side projects, such as curbing and guttering a street that already had those items. We were ecstatic.

The work began. I went out to the site with Chris Lesher, who worked in First Assembly's media department. We were taking film footage of the vacant lot before the excavation and building began. Chris' statement seemed to capture my heart: "You know, Jay, First Assembly has never done anything like this! This is really exciting!" It was! The boys I mentored and the gang that had developed through our days of playing basketball came down that day. We took pictures in front of the lot and then pictures after the construction began.

The day came when it was time to open Metro Worship Center. I got to name the church. The name had so much meaning. For a long time, even before going down to Ives Walk, the term *worship* became very important to me. During the limited opportunities I had to preach or teach, over and over again I taught on the idea of worship.

It was my belief that the church generally defined *worship* in a limited fashion. We called *worship* what occurred prior to the preaching, when we sang songs. Our church's tradition is to be expressive in worship so that some may raise their hands or even dance during this part of the service.

However, I was inspired to search the Scriptures for a more expansive understanding of what worship was. I discovered that the biblical model of worship was so much more than one part of a public service. I developed a worship grid that visually showed that worship had both a private and public aspect.

Scripture reveals that part of worshiping God involves praising Him publicly. (See Hebrews 10:25; 13:15.) Public praise is coming to church and everything we do there. Everything! It is listening to God's Word, praising God through song, giving in offerings—everything we do when we come together.

However, Jesus criticized the Pharisees for being very interested in this part of worship to the neglect of another very important part of worship. (See Luke 11:43.) The Pharisees became centered more on what people thought about them and what their public image was rather than giving time and thought to what God valued.

The second aspect of worship is private devotion. Jesus discussed the necessity of a private prayer closet, a place separated from the public where one would go in private to commune with God. (See Matthew 6:6.) This private devotion is as important as the public praise that is also so very important in Scripture.

I also discovered a verse in the Book of James that spoke to this matter.

> Religion that God our Father accepts as pure and faultless is this: to look after orphans and widows in their distress and to keep oneself from being polluted by the world.
> —JAMES 1:27, NIV

From this scripture it seemed clear to me that worship, both public and private, also required activity that most would not consider worship.

First, in reverse order of James' description, "keep[ing] oneself from being polluted by the world" is worship. I didn't see this as a command to separate from the world but rather to live in a godly way as we go about our daily lives. I gave this example many times: If you are at work and some coworker is telling a dirty joke, but instead of listening you walk away, that act is worship! I am showing God what I think He is worth by obeying His Word!

Second, James describes God-centered service. In James's day the church was responsible for social services. James expressed the importance to God of helping those most vulnerable in their community, widows and orphans.

It occurred to me one day after I began going to Ives Walk that the people living in the neighborhood resembled the kinds of people James described. Most of the women did not have husbands, and they were raising children who did not have fathers.

I was overwhelmed one day after an amazing game of flag football. I had a blast playing with the kids, and it occurred to me that even that activity was worship. I was spending time as a "father" with "orphans," and that was "pure" religion in God's view. My service was centered on God, and meeting the felt needs of others is worship.

When I began to think about naming our facility and all the competing ideas for what the facility would be used for (some thought it would be simply a mentoring center and even called it that), I was convinced that its function would be to serve as a local church. I also wanted it to be a center in the city where all the aspects of worship could occur. Thus, the name Metro Worship Center seemed like an obvious fit. We would have services (i.e., public praise). We would be a facility that encouraged and even served as a place for private devotion (i.e., the prayer closet). We would use it as a discipling center to teach people how to worship God through godly conduct. Finally, we would be a place where God-centered service would occur, and we would encourage the same service outside the facility as well.

Prior to building Metro, however, I traveled around our neighborhood. I found multiple churches of all kinds of different denominations everywhere. This truth burned in my heart: Ives Walk did not need another traditional church. We made up our minds to continue to be a non-traditional church. Our services would continue to be on Thursday evenings. We would not conflict with traditional church times on Sundays and Wednesdays, and we would encourage those we were reaching to attend a local church at the traditional church service times. In this way we could guard against that plague of the church that says that I want my church to grow at the expense of other churches. I hoped that as Metro grew other neighborhood churches would grow as well.

So, we had a name and a plan. Now it was time to occupy our beautiful new facility. We walked with our people from the SLRCC to Metro and captured it on tape. The facility was beautiful, and we had our worship service that night in grand fashion.

I still asked the Lord, Why have me preach in an empty warehouse? I got a little perspective on that. We didn't always have huge crowds at Metro, but we also never had a service where no one came. That day I preached in an empty warehouse to only those people I dreamed would come was simply to prepare me for the days of having to share a message to an age group that ranged in age from babies to the elderly—and to kids who sometimes would not be quiet. Sometimes success was simply measured by getting through the service without too many disruptions. But at least there were kids to be loud. I have never had a service where I had to preach to an empty room. I would have done it; I had already proved that. But instead I got to share with some of those dark faces I had seen in my mind's eye in that vacant warehouse.

CHAPTER 11

LA LESSONS AND
THE LR HOMELESS

MY SENIOR LAW partner, Jim Wallace, often quotes his wife when he is irritated. Pat says, "You are only as little as the things that irritate you." I have to be honest; occasionally some things people would think about our new ministry would irritate me.

One issue that became prevalent was that many of the people from our church who talked with me about the kids and adults that we were reaching thought they were homeless. I never really understood that. I had made it clear that I was reaching out to the Amelia B. Ives *Housing* Projects, not the Amelia B. Ives Homeless Camp. It just showed, in Pat's words, how little I could be though; they obviously meant no harm.

I knew that Little Rock had a homeless population and even heard that some counted in that number were children. I also learned that a good number of the homeless were veterans of our nation's wars, which really troubled me. Probably like most people I looked at people with a sign that said "Will work for food" with a certain amount of skepticism. When I thought of the homeless as a group I had images of the hobo from *The Andy Griffith Show,* who was played by Buddy Ebsen and who tried to get Opie Taylor (Ron Howard) to help him in his freeloading ways.

Then I was invited by Pastor Rod Loy to spend some time with him in Los Angeles at the Dream Center. Matthew Barnett, a young Assemblies of God minister from Phoenix, Arizona, had moved to inner-city LA to plant a church there and was having amazing success. His father, the pastor of Phoenix First Assembly, Tommy Barnett, had been one of my heroes of the faith. The invitation was appreciated. I got to spend time in worship services where Pastor Rod preached and had the opportunity to get to know Matthew and Brother Tommy. It was one of the highlights of my ministry. I also got to meet some of the guys they were ministering to, many of whom had formerly been homeless.

A candle was lit in my heart for the homeless on this venture. I came home not as irritated when someone asked me if we ministered to the homeless.

But it was my second trip to Los Angeles that became another titanic moment. During my second trip to LA I actually stayed at the Dream Center, which is the old Queen of Angels Hospital in downtown LA. The hospital had been donated to Matthew, and they housed the myriad guests who came there to work and minister either short-term or long-term.

This time I got to get out in the streets of LA. I was accompanied by Pastor Tommy Covington, a new pastor on staff that helped us at Metro and who had planted a church in a hospital in Little Rock. His young son, Matt, also came with us.

For anyone interested in ministry, they had a buffet of ministry opportunities. They had ministries that handed out roses to prostitutes at night and gave them an opportunity to leave the street. The police even thanked Matthew and his ministry for shutting down prostitution on several LA streets! What a miracle. They also ministered to the homeless around the LA Union Rescue Mission and an adjoining park. They had bread trucks that would show up in a neighborhood by a school and hand out bread and other kinds of food to people in a line of probably a hundred people. The gentleman who led this ministry trained himself to memorize the names of everyone he served on that particular day. Anytime he met someone new he would memorize his or her name. It was amazing.

Pastor Tommy and I were not allowed to go out at night to minister to the prostitutes because his young son was with us, and I wasn't going without them. But we did participate in the homeless ministry and food distribution.

I will never forget stepping off the bus across the street from the LA Union Rescue Mission. It was a hot day, and the smell of urine on the public street was stifling. We had to sign consents to come because in this part of LA, we were told, it was zoned for the homeless. The city planners had a place where the homeless would be congregated, but the police presence was very low there. The result was an amazingly unpleasant place.

After adjusting to the smell I began to notice the people. I saw a very tired-looking woman and a very large man standing some distance behind her. One of the workers told me to be careful. She was a prostitute, and the big guy was her pimp. I sensed such bondage there, and Pastor Tommy and I could not resist reaching out to the lady. She obviously was in need of ministry, but the guy behind her was very hostile. We stood some distance away and told her we were praying for her. We did, right there. Yet, we both wanted to do so much more. We wanted to see her leave the street. We invited her to attend the worship service the next day.

Then Pastor Tommy, Matt, and I were told that we would be a team. It was our mission just to pray for, get to know, and invite to service the next day anyone that the Lord put in our path. We found a park not far from where the bus was parked. We began to walk through the park and found lots of people lying on blankets. The Union Rescue Mission provides a place for people to sleep at night, and people hang out near the Mission on blankets during the daytime.

As we walked along we saw something that amazed us. There on one of the blankets was a young man and woman with an infant child. Pastor Tommy and I knew this couple was our target. We sat near them and began visiting. We heard their story and learned that this couple and their baby had no place to call their home. They came to LA on a relative's promise of a job and place, but all that fell through. Now they were staying at the Union Rescue Mission at night and in the park during the day. I remember even as I write how the oppressive heat that day made me worry about the life of the baby. We got to know them and simply invited them to church the next day. We told them there would be food and a cool place to stay.

We ministered for well over an hour visiting with people. Quite honestly, I was ready to call it a day. I had seen so many drug deals and so many other acts of lust and violence that I was ready to get back on the bus and head to the Dream Center. We had a moment of comic relief; one guy thought Pastor Tommy was Andre Agassi. He was bald, but I didn't see the resemblance.

Later that day we joined the ministry that loaded bread and fed the homeless. One of the guys working in this ministry was a former NFL football player that Matthew's team found on the streets. He was strung out on drugs. But when they took him in he became a minister there at the Dream Center. They helped him recapture his zest for life, and it didn't hurt that he was an amazingly big and strong guy who no one would mess with.

I was glad as the bus rolled out that this guy was with us. We got to our particular stop, and I was amazed to see what appeared to be at least a hundred people lined up waiting on food. This was not a developing country; this was America. They waited patiently, and we handed out food, toys for kids, and anything else that they had collected. This was their weekly stop, right by an elementary school.

The next morning we went to church hopeful that we might see some of the people we had invited to church. We were not disappointed, because there at the church was the young couple with the infant. This was a significant moment for Pastor Tommy and me and was really the touchstone moment that let us know our time there had not been in vain.

We also walked by Azusa Street, and we saw the location of the great turn-of-the-century revival house. Led by an African-American minister William J. Seymour during the days of Jim Crow segregation, during the Azusa Street Revival people embraced what God was doing and forgot about all the ways they were different. The revival services attracted men, women, and children—black and white, Hispanic, Asian, rich, poor, illiterate, and educated. The Assemblies of God and several other Pentecostal denominations were born during this revival.

After observing ministry to the homeless and desperate and the effectiveness of the ministry in LA, as well as reflecting on the roots of our denomination—which defied racism and gender stereotypes—I came home to Little Rock having learned my LA lessons.

Two weeks later a young man who was working with me during the summer while he was home from Bible school and I began our ministry to Little Rock's homeless. Very much like my first date in Ives Walk, I didn't have much of a plan. At least I did have another person with me. We went to the Salvation Army and just began to visit with people. We learned names and tried to assess the need. After going to Ives Walk on Saturday we found ourselves heading down underneath the Broadway Bridge in Little Rock by the Arkansas River. There we found a whole community of people gathered together. They were homeless, hungry, and some were even anxious to tell us their story.

That first Saturday I met Bob.[2] Bob looked to be the poster boy for some of the Little Rock homeless ministry publications. He looked the part. He had a huge beard, wore a hat on his head, and wore military fatigues and boots. I was shocked at how open he was to share with us his story. The bottom line was that he had a criminal record, which had prevented him from getting employment, and that had robbed him of his self-esteem. He had gone through a divorce with his wife, and he had lost relationships with his four children. Now his goal was simply to survive every day.

I talked to our ministry team, and I also discovered that a couple of people, Bill Lesher and Marianne Harrington, were already making plans to feed the homeless. So, we worked together. A team began meeting on Saturdays at First Assembly and preparing food, and then we would drive it to the Broadway Bridge and feed the homeless.

An amazing team was developing. One day one of our workers, Ronnie Ruple, saw a gentleman who didn't have shoes. He had obviously been beaten up pretty badly the night before and had been robbed of everything, including his shoes. I watched as Ronnie measured his foot and then, certain their feet were the same size, stepped into the guys' house shoes and out of his very nice work boots. Those acts of love and kindness began to penetrate even the hardest hearts.

---

2 This name has been changed.

One day we also met a guy named Phil[3] who told us that Arkansas' first lady, Janet Huckabee, as well as Sandra Wilson, the Homeless Coalition director, had spent the night under the bridge the night before to try to understand what it was like to be homeless. He told us that they were safe, though, as he always slept with a big machete, and he gave us a winning smile. I also met Sandra that day, and she would become an amazing friend to our ministry.

In January of 2004 I was blessed with the arrival of my firstborn, Hallie Claire. Dawn and I were so happy to have this little bundle of joy. Becoming a father also opened my heart up even more to love people the way our heavenly Father loved them.

One day while feeding the homeless I saw a young woman coming for food. She was a mess. Her hair was unkempt, her clothes were dirty, and she looked to be either high or mentally ill. But as we served her the Lord opened my eyes to see her the way He did. I have never heard the audible voice of God, but I clearly heard Him speaking to my heart about this woman.

"Do you know how much you love Hallie?" The question rang in my heart. "That is how much I love my daughter that is standing before you. Will you love her for me?" This question and admonition from the Lord penetrated through my armor. The image of the homeless I needed to serve was no longer from some made-up situation comedy but was now someone I had to love as my own daughter.

---

3   This name has been changed.

I believe it is easy before you know hungry kids or the homeless to view them as a group and dismiss them, but when you begin to learn their names and hear their stories it makes all the difference.

We began a bus route to the homeless for our Thursday night service. We added them to the mix at Metro at seven o'clock every Thursday. We had everyone from infants to grown men in fatigues that came in from the streets. It wasn't quite Azusa Street or the Dream Center, but we were getting closer.

Bob and Phil became regulars. Bob would often come and request prayer for his relationship with his children to be restored. Phil needed a physical healing and better employment. Both became symbols of the homeless ministry to me.

One day Bob disappeared. We heard rumors about him but nothing concrete. One disadvantage of ministry to the homeless is how very transient they can be. I also realized that losing someone from the homeless ministry was probably a good thing. We might have the only ministry model where losing people was valued above gaining him or her. When we lost them it quite often meant they had left the streets.

While we were thinking about Bob, Phil decided he was ready for a life change. We were able to get him housing and a job. His transformation was incredible. He went from a tough, cursing, and bitter guy to a guy who had dedicated his life to Jesus. He was more active, had a tender heart that caused him to cry easily, and got back on his feet financially. Pretty soon a kind person at First Assembly gave him a work truck. He began attending First Assembly and then bought property several counties away from Pulaski County. He started a business, bought land and a house, and began attending a Baptist church in the community.

However, Phil always comes back at Thanksgiving to help us serve our Thanksgiving feast at the Hall of Industry to the homeless and inner-city families.

One day Bob returned to Metro. However, we didn't recognize him. His hat was gone, and so were the army fatigues. He had a haircut and a shave and had on blue jeans. He told us that one of his sons came and told him he couldn't stand for them to be separated any longer. They embraced, forgave each other, and Bob had the reunion with his children for which we had prayed.

About a month later Bob joined the King's Team, which is a ministry discussed below. Bob knew where homeless people were, and he helped us minister to them.

Metro doesn't have a baptistery, so we baptize people at First Assembly. I was never so happy as the night I got to baptize Bob at First Assembly. He gave his testimony, and the before-and-after photographs of Bob were incredible. He looked like a different person.

I will never forget what Bob said that night. He said, "If God can save a wretch like me, He can save anybody!" What an amazing statement.

While Bob and Phil are two success stories, we have had more failures and difficulties with getting people off the streets than we have had successes. We started a couple of ministries, though, aimed at trying to help people transition.

Our Thanksgiving dinner at St. John's got bigger every year, and we began to feed the homeless as well. Starting in 2003 we began having the dinner in the Hall of Industry at the State Fairgrounds. This would become our largest outreach of the year. On the Tuesday before Thanksgiving an incredible team of people led by Krista Dudte would prepare a Thanksgiving feast. But it became so much more than a meal. We began giving out full turkey dinners to every inner-city family head-of-household who was present. We also began putting together care packages for our homeless friends.

We also wanted to see how many service providers we could pack into one room. Since the State of Arkansas was kind enough to donate the use of the Hall of Industry to us, and since it is a very large facility, we had room to fill it with people and services.

We began to provide health services, government services, clothing, haircuts, and a program that became known as Homeless Court. One of our local judges came to the event, along with his bailiff and a prosecutor and public defender. Any homeless person who showed up could get a letter of exoneration to assist them with any subsequent court cases.

We also provided more and more services for kids. We wanted to have fun activities but also services for kids. So, we have given out balloons, clothes, and books and even had special guests, such as Clifford the Big Red Dog, who showed up once.

Being an attorney, I also wanted to emphasize legal assistance at this event. I was so pleased when the Pulaski County, Arkansas Bar Association and the

Center for Arkansas Legal Services began providing free legal advice at this event. Leading the way were partners at my law firm.

I began to see how being an attorney and a minister made sense. Many of the people to whom I was ministering appreciated the fact that I was an attorney as much as the fact that I was a minister.

I began studying Jesus' role for believers, which is described in the Scriptures as that of an advocate. I came to realize that Jesus' role before God, our Judge, was that of a defense attorney. The devil was the prosecutor, pointing out all of our faults and defects. Jesus, on the other hand, defended us in our weakness. When I discovered this role Jesus plays I saw the practice of law in more sacred terms.

METRO CAFÉ AND KING'S TEAM

Before long we developed a vision for taking what we did once a year with the Thanksgiving outreach and multiplying those efforts so that we could gather once a month. I also had a friend who believed his ministry was preparing food. Earlier in his life Bill Lesher had fed people in need at another church and since that time had dreamed of doing so at First Assembly.

For some time Bill had been preparing the food that we took to feed the homeless on Saturdays. However, we envisioned opening a free restaurant for the homeless where they could come and be served while sitting at a table. We realized that most of the times the homeless were fed they stood in line for the food. We wanted to make them feel like cherished patrons of a fine restaurant. That desire led to the opening of Metro Café, our homeless restaurant at Metro Worship Center. Bill and an amazing team of food preparers and servers began serving food one Saturday every month.

Like the Thanksgiving outreach, we determined to provide services also. While the services were more limited than Thanksgiving, on various Saturdays most of the same services are provided.

Recently a local dry-cleaners just gave us mountains of clothes that they had pressed and cleaned. Metro has a clothes room, and with this addition the goal of clothing people has continued and expanded.

A need that arose from Metro Café, however, was getting the word out about the free restaurant. For some time I had dreamed of having a ministry like some of those I saw in Los Angeles where we could go out and perform street ministry.

Earlier at Metro we formed a team called the King's Team. It was the duty of this team to invite people to come to Metro on Thursday nights by handing out flyers door to door.

This idea was revived and used to target the homeless and prostitutes in Little Rock. The night before Metro Café, Friday nights, I would lead a team to different homeless camps and areas with high prostitution. We would hand out food and water to everyone, along with flyers about the next day's Metro Café and the multiple bus routes that we would run. Then we would give a single red rose to any lady we found on the street.

The King's Team took on a life of its own. The King's Team would meet for prayer from 8:30 to 9:30, and then the outreach would occur from 9:30 until midnight. Multiple salvations have occurred during this event. One of our stops is at a liquor store on Asher Avenue in Little Rock. We are not there to preach to people going in the liquor store. Actually, we are grateful for a place to park, as there are homeless guys on the street corner near the liquor store. One particular night a guy pulled up in a car and saw our church bus. He said he had been trying to run from God all day, and now he couldn't even find any relief at the liquor store. Weeping openly, he surrendered his life to the Lord in the liquor store parking lot. Over and over again people gave their hearts to Jesus and their Saturday lunchtime the next day to Metro Café.

In the New Testament Jesus tells a story about a king who is having a wedding feast for his son. He prepares an amazing feast, but those he invited refused to come. Indignant, the king sent his servants out to find others who could come. Matthew 22:9 (NIV) says, "So go to the street corners and invite to the banquet anyone you find." While this was a parable of Jesus about the kingdom of heaven, we decided to take this story literally. Jesus is the King of kings and Lord of lords. So, He is the King. We are His servants—thus, His team. At Metro we have a literal banquet—plenty of food and goods for the homeless. However, we also have a figurative banquet, the kind that the spirit of the homeless needs—a community of people who love them and who will point those who are far from Christ toward Him.

We continued to dream of ways to touch the homeless in central Arkansas. One ministry we began was reading the Bible to the homeless on the streets. On Monday and Thursday mornings, usually reading only one chapter at a time, I have read through the entire New Testament and much of the Old Testament to a group of homeless that meet there at those times in the River Market in downtown Little Rock. I arrive at 8:30 a.m., read the Bible without comment, pray, and then head to my law office. It is a great way to start the work week and a great way to begin our Thursday outreach.

Now when people ask if I minister to the homeless I say yes. That is one of the groups of people to whom we minister. My mind has been changed about the homeless, and I have even come to identify with them.

Our Lord described Himself as homeless. In Luke 9:57–58 (NIV) Jesus has an interesting dialogue with a man who would have been a follower: "As they were walking along the road, a man said to him, 'I will follow you wherever you go.' Jesus replied, 'Foxes have dens and birds have nests, but the Son of Man has no place to lay his head.'" Jesus had been a carpenter and no doubt earned a living doing so. Jesus also had contributors to His ministry. Yet, Jesus chose to spend much of His ministry years traveling from town to town and living outside. Some have argued that Jesus was homeless; I think it is clear that Jesus chose to live without the comfort of a home.

I learned that some people choose homelessness, just like Jesus. I met an evacuee from Hurricane Katrina who fled New Orleans, Louisiana, when that dreaded hurricane destroyed the city. Yet, he rejected opportunities to return to his home, feeling instead called to

Little Rock to live and minister among the homeless as someone who is homeless. He often joins us when I read the Bible in the River Market, and he often prays also. He has a rich relationship with the Lord and chooses homelessness.

Most, however, do not choose homelessness. For many, like Bob, a series of poor choices, criminal records, and drugs and alcohol lead to a loss of family and resources. Having nowhere else to turn, many become homeless and learn how to survive that way.

Many are also veterans, people who served our nation during times of war. Now, due to Post-Traumatic Stress Disorder or other mental illnesses or problems, they find themselves homeless.

I was asked once what questions we ask or how we qualify people for the assistance we provide. In explaining that we were not the government and did not have to attempt to qualify people I also said that anyone who asks for help gets it. We don't try to determine whether people are on the streets for some legitimate reason or not. We merely minister to them.

Jesus did not put qualifications on providing for the physical needs of people. In dividing the sheep from the goats one day Jesus will simply ask, "How did you treat the hungry, the thirsty, the stranger, those needing clothes, the sick, and the incarcerated?" If you ministered to their needs, you ministered to Jesus. But if you looked the other way, you failed to minister to Jesus. (See Matthew 25:31–46.)

CHAPTER 12

IVES WALK, SUNSET, AND THE TEN MOST CHALLENGED NEIGHBORHOODS IN LITTLE ROCK

As the ministry in Ives Walk continued to grow we also began partnering more and more with the Little Rock Housing Authority. An employee there approached me one day with a request: "Can you begin something in Sunset Terrace like what you are doing in Ives Walk?"

First we were flattered that a representative of the city would ask for our assistance. Next we started dreaming of expanding to a second neighborhood.

The first thing we did was pray. First Assembly's student minister, Pastor John Van Pay, and I led a busload of students to Sunset Terrace one Saturday to simply walk around the neighborhood and pray. Unfortunately the huge school bus we were in died on the way up Roosevelt Hill before we could arrive at Sunset Terrace.

So, with the skill of a professional driver, Pastor John backed the huge bus into the gas station at the bottom of the hill. It turns out that we were out of gas. This seemed so fitting for one of my projects. We unloaded the kids, I stood with them on the hill, and Pastor John gassed up the bus. After reloading our students we drove to Sunset Terrace.

The prayer time was rich. The students asked why we were just praying. We explained the request and our desire to make a difference in this neighborhood. However, we told them that every project must begin with prayer.

About a month later I was in Sunset Terrace with a team going door to door to invite people to Metro's Thursday night service. One young lady who answered the door seemed shocked. She said, "It seems to me that you are on some kind of a crusade!" I told her she was absolutely right.

Soon we had a core of students and a few adults who rode a bus to Metro every Thursday. We included outreach to Sunset on Saturdays as well. And soon one of my friends who had been helping in Ives Walk, Carl Culpepper, became Pastor Carl. He became to Sunset Terrace what I had become to Ives Walk! He loved the kids there, and they loved him.

The ministry to our second neighborhood was going very well. Then our next challenge came, not from the city but from the Lord. I wrestled with the fact that the kids in Sunset Terrace were just like the ones in Ives Walk. They were so vulnerable. They had time on their hands. Over and over again, throughout the city, there were housing projects where there were students and kids who needed an outreach ministry. Then the mission became engraved on our hearts: reach the ten most challenged neighborhoods in Little Rock.

The task was large. After all, we were doing well to minister adequately to Ives Walk and Sunset Terrace. Yet, the knowledge that there were kids all over the city with physical and spiritual needs continued to motivate us to pray and study other opportunities.

One day I began to visit with a Little Rock police officer who attended First Assembly. I asked him if he could help me understand where the highest crime areas were in the city. Soon he became a partner in understanding where the hardest to reach areas of our city were.

The goal became simple: every summer we would pray about starting a presence in one or two new neighborhoods. Then we would work toward incorporating the neighborhood into another one of our ministry areas.

Our first summer we settled on Eastview Terrace in the Hangar Hill community and Pebble Creek Apartments in Southwest Little Rock. Eastview Terrace made sense from a geographical standpoint in that it was only about five miles from Metro. However, Pebble Creek was about fourteen miles from Metro and was further than we initially felt led to extend the ministry. Yet, I had grown up in Southwest Little Rock and had graduated from McClellan High School. McClellan was about a mile from Pebble Creek. Many of the students that lived in Pebble Creek attended McClellan.

We decided to make our first appearance in these neighborhoods big. We set up huge cookouts, gave out back-to-school supplies, and held a full, outside religious service in three venues: Sunset Terrace, Eastview Terrace, and Pebble Creek. We had music, had a human video with the music, and Pastor Steve and I spoke. We drew a huge crowd at all places, and it was clear that we had invaded new ground.

Pastor Steve and I also almost had heat strokes, as the August heat was almost unbearable.

Soon we started bus routes to these two new neighborhoods. We were also thrilled that one of our leaders, Bart Perrier, felt called to Pebble Creek. I had gone to high school with Bart, and I learned that he had lived in Pebble Creek Apartments while attending school there. He felt like he had just returned home. He ministered in amazing ways to the neighborhood.

Eastview Terrace also became the grounds for one of our summer mentoring activities. With the assistance of the apartment complex owners, we gained access to a multi-purpose room there, and one of our schoolteacher volunteers, Carol, led a mentoring program for students there.

With the addition of new neighborhoods we were thrilled to find more students we could help. We also learned that Ives Walk was being torn down. The buildings had become old, and both the upper and lower projects were removed. When I learned this was happening I was very sad. After all, this was the original neighborhood to which I had been called. Yet, I understood the call to the ten most challenged neighborhoods now.

As we went to Sunset Terrace, Eastview Terrace, and Pebble Creek we learned that some of our friends in

Ives Walk had to move to one of these new areas. It was described once as the diaspora. They were sent out, and what occurred was that they knew Metro and us; therefore we had friends waiting on us in the new neighborhoods to which we were being called.

The next summer we went to the original neighborhood the Little Rock Police officer identified as one of the most challenged areas in our city, Kanis Point. We added to Kanis Point an apartment complex not too far away on Thirty-Sixth Street called Fair Oaks Apartments. These two apartment complexes would make up our Barrow Road ministry.

With each new neighborhood we needed additional volunteers to both have a presence in the neighborhood and also to bring our new friends to Metro by bus on Thursday nights.

I often felt that trying to reach the ten most challenged neighborhoods was a task that was larger than our volunteer capacity. We were in five neighborhoods—halfway there—and I felt the same way I felt when I discovered so many students in Ives Walk. It was the realization that we had to keep expanding in volunteers in order to minister adequately to our new neighborhoods.

However, one of my favorite poets had a good perspective on the faith life. Robert Browning said, "Ah, but a man's reach should exceed his grasp, or what's a heaven for?"

We marched on. The next summer we followed one of our new volunteers, Pastor Otis, to his old neighborhood, Woodhaven Apartments off of Geyer Springs Road in Southwest Little Rock. We also reached out to his new apartment complex, Berwyn Square Apartments on Sixty-Fifth Street. These were both small apartment complexes, and with Otis's influence we had an immediate impact on both neighborhoods.

We continued to minister to the new neighborhoods on Saturdays, much like I did in the beginning in Ives Walk. Since we had additional neighborhoods we had to expand our teams to reach out. We called the Saturday ministry Adopt-A-Block. We tried to simply have fun on Saturdays. We also tried to meet needs in the community.

With the help of Bill Lesher and a generous barbeque restaurant in North Little Rock, pretty soon we were handing out barbeque in our neighborhoods. As a matter of fact, in Pebble Creek I became known as the barbeque man. I thought that was probably a more effective handle than "pastor."

We continued for the next two summers to add our final two neighborhoods. The first were the St. John Apartments, which were across the street from Berwyn Square on Sixty-Fifth Street. We also opened Spring Valley Apartments at Interstate 30 and Geyer Springs.

While our volunteers are incredible and we are impacting our new neighborhoods, recently I began a project to determine every apartment complex in Little Rock where people receive government assistance for housing. The reason is that I know there are students throughout Little Rock who need us, who need the Lord, and who need Metro Worship Center.

Our reach is still greater than our grasp, and my fear is becoming "a mile long and an inch deep." Yet, I know that the volunteers will come. We also need pastors to give their lives to neighborhoods and apartment complexes.

One of our leaders, Pastor Steve Flores, recently left North Little Rock and moved his wife and two young children to the neighborhood near Kanis Point. Pastor Steve feels a special identification with this neighborhood. My prayer is that more people will feel called to each of our neighborhoods and neighborhoods we have not yet reached.

CHAPTER 13

METRO REFLECTIONS

ONE OF MY fears in writing this book is leaving out the names of key people who were with me in the beginning, or who helped lead. So, I asked several of those key people to write a paragraph or two about their reflections on the birth of Metro Worship Center and our ministry.

The next few pages are in the words of some of the most amazing people I have come to know. Some are mothers of students we reached; others are the actual students, many of whom are all grown up. Many are key leaders.

Their words will allow me to finish the task of sharing my transformation from lawyer to lawyer/pastor.

As you read their words I also want you to know that your steps of faith will produce similar people in your life. Some of the most rich and amazing relationships you will have in your life will occur as you step out in faith like Abram, like Moses, and like Jesus, our Lord and Savior. God's heroes are still being called. I am not a hero—just a servant—but the people whose words you are about to read are heroes. Your obedience can help make the lives of others clearer and can prompt special obedience to the Lord in amazing ways.

My challenge to you is this: Take the first step. Do that thing you have been called to do. Join my friends and me. Do it now!

KRISTA DUDTE

One day in our Sunday school class at church Jay Martin spoke about an inner-city ministry in which he was involved. He talked about playing football on Saturdays in the Ives Walk neighborhood. My husband, Robb, felt moved to volunteer on a Saturday to investigate. Robb started going on Thursday nights to the Bible study Jay led at the community center. Robb told me that I should go one Thursday night to see what it was about.

Our son, Joshua, was twenty months old at the time. My honest first thought was that I didn't want to take my baby "down to the 'hood." In the spring of 2000 Joshua and I went to Bible study one Thursday night. The first night I was there I met a boy named Jasper Brown who turned around the entire service looking at Joshua and me. I held Joshua on my lap while kids would come up to him, and one child even broke a couple of his crayons.

I went home that night thinking about the kids and my baby's broken crayons. But I could not get Jasper's face out of my head. I knew then that God was speaking to me about Ives Walk. I can't explain it into words other than that God changed my heart for Ives Walk and the kids at the community center.

Robb, Joshua, and I began going to Bible study every Thursday night. A few months later I became pregnant with Bethany. I felt accepted when the women from the neighborhood threw me a surprise baby shower.

In March 2001 Bethany was born, and in May 2001 Metro Worship Center opened. Bethany, at six weeks old, and I waited there while Jay led the others on a walk from the Community Center to Metro Worship Center for the opening.

Thursday nights were a family event for a while for us. Bethany would crawl around Metro while Jay preached. She was passed around the neighborhood women like a baby doll. Robb eventually started staying home on Thursday nights so I could devote my attention to what needed to be done at Metro. It wasn't always easy with two little ones.

Later on I became pregnant with Samuel. I went to Metro Thursday night and had Samuel three days later. Life was hard at times, and still is with the kids, schedules, and homework. They know that it isn't an option. Mom goes to Metro, and most of the time they come as well. It is a second home to us, as well as the people there. The people there are our family. It's not about me, my discomfort, or my kid's discomfort. I know that God called me to go to Metro. I'm so thankful He did.

JASPER BROWN

My name is Jasper Brown, and I am twenty-one years old. I grew up living in the Amelia B. Ives Housing Projects. My neighborhood was one of the roughest neighborhoods in Little Rock. I grew up surrounded by violence and witnessing many bad things. I met Pastor Jay Martin when I was six years old. He came to my house and invited me and my family to Metro Worship Center, a church he started in my neighborhood. At that time it was located in the South Little Rock Community Center, where all of us hung out after school. When I went to Metro I did not know what to expect but came with an open mind.

I met a lady named Krista Dudte, who I became very fond of. She guided me to a room where they held Bible study. I began to meet more people I liked. I enjoyed the services and particularly the singing. I attended Metro then and still attend today.

If it wasn't for a church like Metro being in my neighborhood and meeting someone like Pastor Jay, who took me under his wings, I would have fallen into the wrong crowds and possibly ended up in jail.

Instead I graduated from Little Rock Central High School with a 3.2 grade point average, and I currently attend Pulaski Technical College, where I am majoring in criminal justice.

I am so thankful that the Lord used Pastor Jay to begin a ministry to help a kid like me, keep me off the streets, and help me continue my education.

MARIANNE HARRINGTON

When Pastor Jay asked me to jot down some things about my involvement with the homeless ministry I had to go way back to the beginning of when a calling was placed on my life in my teenage years. I was raised Catholic and was privileged to have twelve years of Catholic education and church-going. The one thing I remember very clearly was a love I had for God and a close relationship with the Lord. I loved Jesus, and it seemed I prayed a child's prayer for His love in my life.

As I progressed in my school years my relationship with the Lord deepened. I loved to go to chapel and just be in prayer with Him. I felt a calling to be a missionary and to serve the Lord as a teacher or nurse. I made a decision that I wanted to serve Him totally and completely. I must have been about fifteen years old when I made a decision to enter the convent. I had dreams of winning people over to the Lord. One of the sisters became my mentor, and we spent time in discussion of God's will in my life. I became a servant in volunteering my time to the poor and the elderly.

I remember approaching my mother when I was seventeen years old to tell her of my plans for my life, to enter the convent and to become a nun, and I remember her response: "Before you make a decision like that you need to experience the world." My parents felt I was too young and inexperienced to make a decision that would have such a profound effect on my life. I went on to nursing school—public—and began to "experience the world," as my mom stated. This was the beginning of my fall from grace. But it was also the beginning of another miracle in my life, one that would take years to complete.

There was a history of alcoholism in my family, and things got pretty bad while I was in nursing school. I can remember times when I avoided visiting members of my family until after I was sure they had passed out. Interestingly enough, I followed right in those footsteps. I managed to graduate from nursing school in spite of my dope-smoking, speed-taking, and drinking-stupor escapades. It is only through the miracle of God that I did not become addicted to drugs or alcohol myself.

By 2000 I had established a career in nursing, was married, and had two children. Then I found myself divorced and without my mom and dad, who both had passed away. However, even with loss, over the years I had grown in my relationship with my God.

I remember that back in the early '80s when I was still working as a nurse in psychiatry the hospital where I worked decided to close beds. We were given a list of areas that had openings, and according to seniority we could select where we wanted to work. By the time it came down to me there were positions open only in the drug-and-alcohol unit. I could not believe it; the one place I had no desire to work because of my family history is where I would have to work. I remember the nuns telling us, "You can't hate anyone; dislike, yes, but we are not capable of hating." At that moment in my life I thought, "How wrong they were." I despised alcoholics and drug addicts.

The hurt from my dad resurfaced, this time full-blown. I had never dealt with the hurts of my youth. I could not stand to even think about working with these people who I thought at that time were the scum of the earth. I remember the assistant chief nurse telling me, "Marianne, you would work great with these people. You're such a caring nurse." She did not know my history. She kept prodding me to accept a position until one day I had had enough. I remember breaking down and spilling my guts about my dad. I told her that if they put me on the drug-and-alcohol unit they would have a patient abuse case against me. The first time one of those drunks gave me a sob story I would tell them where to get off. Well, I did not go to the drug-and-alcohol unit, so I was able to suppress those hurts one more time.

In the early '90s I started attending church at First Assembly of God, North Little Rock, Arkansas. I became involved in the singles group after my divorce in '97. Around 2001 I went to the Dream Center in Los Angeles with the singles from the church. I thought it would be a lot of fun to go. It was more than that. It was a heart-changing experience for me. God softened my heart and healed the hurts related to an alcoholic father. It was then that I really understood that all people, no matter what their circumstance, were children of God, and it was truly God's desire that all would come to know Him. I had a calling on my life as teenager, a calling that had never left me, a calling to be a missionary and in service to the Lord. God is an awesome God. He has never forsaken me. He does not see me as unworthy to do His work.

It is because of that trip, the prayers of many, and the faithfulness of my loving, heavenly Father that I am involved in the homeless ministry. When Pastor Jay announced that First Assembly was creating a homeless ministry I was over-joyed to become involved. It is fulfillment for me, being used by God to further His kingdom. I will tell you that being involved in the ministry for approximately nine years has had its ups and downs. Seeing people come to Christ has been a slow process. Probably the most memorable event of the ministry for me was when James C. asked me to be in the baptismal tank when he was baptized! One of the most heartbreaking was seeing Dale fall off the wagon, wind up on the street again, and eventually die on that street. There have been some I know who have come to the Lord and deepened their relationship with Him, and then there have been some who use the ministry as a place of warmth and food for a short time, and that's it!

There are many reasons I have observed for people to be homeless: poor choices in life, unfortunate circumstances, addictions, and mental illness. It is not for me to judge; it is only for me to show these individuals the love of Christ. In that way their hearts may be softened and receptive to the Holy Spirit.

It seems so important that we listen for God's voice to guide us and mold us. God will take us places we never dreamed of or thought possible. He will provide us the means, the talents, and the abilities to minister to people who He wants in loving relationship with Him. God blesses me with peace. My hope is that others can truly experience God's blessing in their lives when they are in full and committed relationship with Him. We serve an awesome God who truly loves us and wants to bless us always.

JAMES C.

My first memory of Metro's ministry was being fed under the Broadway Bridge in Little Rock, where

I was living. I had been living on the streets for twenty-five years at that time and was in a wheelchair. I had given up and didn't care. That was why I was homeless. I met Marianne Harrington and Ronnie Ruple and his daughters. They would come up and hug my leg and let me know they had been thinking about me and praying for me during the week. Since I had been separated from my kids for thirty years, the interaction with Ronnie's girls allowed them to take my kids' place. Ronnie would also take me over to his house, where I could bathe. For a couple of years I was fed on Saturdays under the Broadway Bridge.

At some point during this time I also began riding the bus to Metro Worship Center for their Thursday night services. One Thursday night at Metro I rededicated my life to the Lord and was baptized at First Assembly.

After having hope restored in my life I made up my mind to leave the streets. I also no longer needed to use my wheelchair. Ronnie helped me get a job cutting poles for the railroad. During this job I camped out on the tracks for another year. Then, after saving up some money, I bought a house. My job took me a hundred miles from Central Arkansas. While I now cut down trees and mow yards rather than working for the railroad, I still live in the house I am purchasing. I got involved in a local church and return to Central Arkansas once per month.

I was also excited to join ministry opportunities through Metro Worship Center, including the King's Team and also the Thanksgiving outreach. Having been on the streets and going out and ministering, I believe if God helps you get off the street, you kind of need to pay back. I enjoy sharing how God has changed me and have done so on a local news program, where I was interviewed during my service at a Thanksgiving outreach. I just told her that it is good to see people ministering to the homeless as long as their motive is that of love and not just to look good. If the motives are wrong the homeless can recognize that, and the good that is done is diminished.

One of the things I am most excited about is the food ministry I have been able to start in the community in which I live. Bill Lesher gives me an ice chest full of food, and I take it up there and give it to the single moms in my community. Having been homeless and now being able to feed others is a blessing. The people I feed are young mothers who have very little, with the fathers not caring or coming around. I try to help them out the best I can.

One final thing: Having been homeless, it is very important for young people to get involved in homeless ministry. I was most impacted by the young who reached out to me.

Bill Lesher with Glenda Lesher

For I was hungry and you gave me something to eat.

—Matthew 25:35

In 1984 the Holy Spirit was dealing with a few friends and me about the growing number of street people in the Little Rock area. Homeless, hopeless, and hungry, they wandered the streets of the city looking for a handout, a scrap of food, or any leftover alcohol in a discarded bottle or can.

With the permission and support of the church we were members of at the time we got together with our wives for prayer about the direction we should take. Before long the Sunday morning breakfast program was born. We had drivers that would scout out the hangouts and the dumpsters and bring the men back to the church kitchen. Awaiting them would be coffee and a hot, hearty breakfast served by volunteers. We not only fed them but engaged them in conversation about their lives and their needs. We didn't give them money but gave them something eternal, the gospel. Counseling was also available, as well as hygiene products and clothing. It was not required that they go to church, but they were welcomed and encouraged to.

A change in my life became apparent in 1990. After ten years at that non-denominational church it appeared that ongoing internal problems were getting worse not better. My wife and I made the difficult decision that it was time for us to leave.

We landed at First Assembly of God in North Little Rock, a church that was known for its stableness and continuous growth since its inception in 1912 or so. At first I thought I would just rest on my laurels, heal from wounds, and let others feed me for a change. However, the Lord and Pastor Alton Garrison had other plans. It wasn't long before I was doing volunteer cooking for the church.

It was inevitable that I would get back into the homeless ministry at some point, but working and raising a family took priority for a few years. The leadership of Jay Martin gave me the opportunity and the renewed enthusiasm to jump back in. By then we had a new pastor, Rod Loy, and he had a passion for serving the community. We started feeding the homeless in 2003. This program was completely different from the one I had previously been involved with. We took the food to them! We started cooking lunch in the church kitchen on a Saturday morning and then transporting it to a downtown area where the homeless gather. That continues to this day, and we added a Thursday night sack lunch.

As planner and chief cook I like to make sure that a hot and nutritious meal is served to the homeless people. Amazingly, I found out that they love salad, as not many churches bring that. Things have changed with the homeless population too. It's not just men anymore. Sadly, we see whole families who are down on their luck.

I'm thankful for a compassionate church that underwrites the cost of the groceries and for the many volunteers who help cook, transport meals, and people and who take a personal interest in treating the homeless as people that God loves, not just a project. Feeding them God's Word is just as important as feeding them food.

About fourteen years ago First Assembly decided it was time to place a mission in the east part of Little Rock, an area in decline. The building allowed us to have a church service on Thursday nights for the homeless or anyone who wanted to attend from that area, and also a children's outreach.

Later Metro Café was introduced. From working in restaurants in my youth I know how much people enjoy being served, but the homeless are not financially able to enjoy what many of us take for granted. Metro Café gave us the opportunity to bless others by having a table-service meal once a month. The people are served as if they were paying.

The fruit of giving both spiritual and physical food for the hungry and outcasts of this world have been tremendous. Though not everyone is saved from a life of alcohol and drugs, many have been. If only one, it would be worth it because giving in the name of Jesus is giving to Him.

TERRI LEWIS

When Pastor Jay came into our life—my children, Anthony, Tory, Raven, and Nathaniel, as well as myself—we were in a place where we went to church, but we never had a connection. We just wanted to serve God, and we wanted to learn how to love, serve, and help others. So, when Pastor Jay Martin came to the Ives Walk community he came with Jesus all over him. We were welcome each and every time to come to the Thursday night services. My children enjoyed the Saturday football, as well as basketball games.

Then Pastor Jay started coming with mentors for the children. We were blessed with the Dudte family and Mrs. Alice and Kane Dorsey.

My children and myself grew with our relationship with Jesus! We were able to understand what it was Jesus had for us to do: help and reach out to others. For this reason my family started coming, including my sisters, my mom, aunts, cousins, and friends!

Metro Worship Center means the world to me and my family! My kids and I attend Metro, and now I have grandkids attending!

My kids now help with the younger generation, and my grandchildren love SLAM [the kids' ministry].

I can go on and on and on about how Metro Worship Center saved me, saved my family.

I'm just thankful for Pastor Jay Martin having a heart to help the needy because a lot of families were helped, souls were saved, and hearts were filled because of this man of God. Thank you, Pastor Jay, for having a vision for a community that could have been lost.

Metro Worship Center is my home, a place where you can feel love, peace, and comfort from all the other pastors as well.

MONTEZ PORTER

As a child growing up in the projects it was always hard for me to keep my head up and keep moving forward because of all the things that were happening. Growing up in a single-mother neighborhood, we all had challenges financially and emotionally. The one thing that kept us going as a neighborhood and me as a young man was seeing Pastor Jay keep his word to all of us who came out to play football. Not only did he continue to come out and build a relationship with us, he started a Bible study church called Metro. I can remember the first day that we saw the building we were having church at the center on

Main Street. It was totally shocking to see that we finally had our own building that we could worship and have fellowship in.

Without Metro I can honestly say I don't know exactly where I would be right now because it stopped me from doing a lot of the things that I was doing. It kept me from getting in trouble and helped me build a relationship with all the members of First Assembly and most importantly the Metro staff. I went from being a member to being a full-fledged worker for both of our services, and I couldn't be more satisfied with my life at this moment. Because of Pastor Jay's love not only for me but also for kids in general Metro has become the biggest part in my life when it comes to volunteer work. I am thankful for all Metro has done for me and all the kids that the church continues to reach. It let me know that someone cares about kids like me and our families. I wouldn't change one thing in my life because of the influence that the church has played in my life, and as long as I live I will try my best to work and give back like Pastor Jay and Metro have done for me.

ABOUT THE AUTHOR

LIKE MANY YOUNG people, Jay Martin struggled with his calling. His was an unconventional calling—to be a lawyer and a pastor. During law school, while working for a judge who was also a pastor, Jay found a path that combined the two.

Jay has several passions—his wife of twenty-one years, Dawn, and his three daughters, Hallie, Karis, and Sloane! He is also a basketball and soccer coach for the teams on which Karis and Sloane, his nine-year-old twins, play; a pepper farmer; and he runs marathons.

But his greatest passion is following Jesus Christ. He enjoys leading Metro Worship Center, the inner-city church he planted eighteen years ago, and helping people discover God's plan for their lives. He also enjoys helping people find how to use their professions and skills to serve others.

He dreams of seeing people who will serve as mentors and friends to kids without dads flock to the inner city, trailer parks, and challenged neighborhoods in their cities! He believes the answer to racial reconciliation in our country is simply Christ-followers sharing His love and building personal relationships. He hopes his life has provided an example of one way this can occur, and he challenges folks, particularly young people, to impact the life of even one child!

CONTACT THE AUTHOR

JAY MARTIN MAY be reached by e-mail at hcm@ wallacelawfirm.com or by phone at (501) 375-5545. Mail may be directed to his attention at:

212 Center Street
Suite 100, First Floor Centre Place Bldg.
Little Rock, Arkansas 72201

Visit Metro Worship Center on Facebook at https:// www.facebook.com/MetroWorshipCenter/.